# SIR THOMAS WYATT

*AND*

## SOME COLLECTED STUDIES

# SIR THOMAS WYATT

*AND*

## SOME COLLECTED STUDIES

By

E. K. CHAMBERS

*New York*

RUSSELL & RUSSELL

1965

FIRST PUBLISHED IN 1933

REISSUED, 1965, BY RUSSELL & RUSSELL, INC.

BY ARRANGEMENT WITH SIDGWICK & JACKSON, LTD., LONDON

L. C. CATALOG CARD NO: 65—13939

PRINTED IN THE UNITED STATES OF AMERICA

# CONTENTS

*page*

*Prefatory Note* vii

Some Points in the Grail Legend 1

Sir Thomas Malory 21

Some Aspects of Mediæval Lyric 46

Sir Thomas Wyatt 98

The English Pastoral 146

The Disenchantment of the Elizabethans 181

*Appendix*
  The Court of Venus 207

# PREFATORY NOTE

THESE papers are a gathering from many years. *The English Pastoral* was prefixed to an anthology made for Messrs Blackie and Son in 1895, and my thanks are due to the publishers for leave to reprint it. *Some Aspects of Mediæval Lyric* was written for *Early English Lyrics*, compiled by Mr Frank Sidgwick and me in 1907. *Sir Thomas Malory* was read to the English Association in 1922 and issued by them as a pamphlet. *Some Points in the Grail Legend* was read to the Arthurian Society of Oxford in 1928, and appeared in their *Arthuriana*. *Sir Thomas Wyatt* and the little lecture on the Elizabethans have not been printed before.

E. K. C.

# SOME POINTS in the GRAIL LEGEND

I DO not propose to achieve the quest of the Grail. That mysterious vessel has stood for different things to different men, and its history opens many doors into mediæval thought and literature. Unfortunately, progress is barred by the fact that the earliest texts relating to it still need a critical editor; and I have myself no competence in Celtic or continental tongues.[1]

I shall, therefore, mainly concern myself with some speculations as to the original conception which underlies the first appearance of the Grail in romance. And I shall assume that we have little means of arriving at that conception, except through an interpretation of Chrétien de Troyes, and perhaps his earliest continuators; that the later continuators, the verse of Robert de Boron, the prose romances, and the German and Welsh versions only represent attempts to fill out a story which the *Conte del Graal* had left imperfect; and that the Grail was not originally linked with the adventures of Perceval le Gallois. Many of these assumptions are disputable, and I am not sure that they are all sound. In particular, the obscure references of Wolfram von Eschenbach to a writer he calls Kyot may indicate some knowledge of a version which

[1] For Chrétien's share see now the edition of A. Hilka (1932).

I

goes behind Chrétien. But whether that is so or not, I do not think that it much affects what I shall have to discuss.

I do not see how the Grail can be of Christian origin. But in Chrétien it is already to some extent Christianised. It is a holy and spiritual thing, and in it is a Host, by which the father of the lord of the Grail Castle is nourished. One cannot, of course, with that ardent Celticist, Professor Brown, treat the Host, without any authority from the known manuscripts, as an interpolation, merely because it is left out of the printed prose version of 1530; even though there is manuscript authority for so treating the introduction, in a later passage not written by Chrétien, of Joseph of Arimathea. I take it that Chrétien meant in some way to link up the Grail with one of those Holy Blood relics, which were common enough in the Middle Ages. Miss Weston supposes this to have been a Holy Blood at Fécamp; surely perversely, since there was also, and still is, a famous Holy Blood at Bruges, brought there in the second crusade, and at Bruges ruled Philip of Alsace, Count of Flanders, for whom Chrétien wrote. The book which Count Philip gave to Chrétien for the purposes of his poem is more likely to have been a legend of this than an earlier Grail romance. No doubt Chrétien had also such a romance, as well as one of Perceval, if indeed the two had not already been linked.

The story, as told by Chrétien, is, of course, familiar, and if I summarise it, it is merely for the sake of comparing the details of its Grail visit with those in the early continuations.

Perceval has left his forest home, visited Arthur's court, slain the Red Knight who took the cup from the royal board, and won the love of Blancheflor. These early adventures have nothing to do with the Grail, except that in the course of them an old knight warns Perceval not to be too talkative and inquisitive. Leaving Blancheflor in her castle, he rides to seek his mother. He reaches a river, where is a man fishing in a boat, who promises to lodge him for the night. He rides on to a castle. An old man is lying on a couch in a crowded hall. A squire enters, bearing a sword, on which is written that it will only break in one peril, known to him alone who forged it, and he alone can mend it. The host gives Perceval the sword, as judged and destined for him. A procession enters the hall. A valet carries a lance, from the point of which a drop of blood runs down to his hand. Perceval, remembering the warning of the old knight, asks no question. Two more valets bear gold candlesticks. A damsel brings a Grail, also of gold, adorned with precious stones, and the brightness which comes from it outshines the candles. Last comes one with a silver carving dish. The procession crosses the hall, passing from chamber to chamber. Again Perceval refrains from asking whom they served from the Grail. A meal follows. A valet carves on the silver dish. At each course the Grail passes again. And Perceval is still silent. He goes to bed,

3

and, waking on the morrow, finds the castle deserted and his horse and armour awaiting him. As he rides over the drawbridge, it is raised, so suddenly that he hardly escapes. In the forest he finds a maiden, who declares herself his cousin. She tells him that his host was the rich Fisher King, who has been wounded through the thighs in battle, and fishes for relaxation. If he had asked about the lance and Grail, the King would have been healed, and much good would have come of it. The sword will fail Perceval in need, and must be mended by dipping in a lake where its maker, Trebuchet, lives. Perceval returns to Arthur's camp. Thither comes a loathly damsel, and repeats the reproaches of Perceval's cousin. His failure means death for knights, woe for wives, and shame for maidens in the Fisher's land. Perceval vows himself to the quest of the Grail.

Now Chrétien follows the adventures not of Perceval, but of Gawain, in the midst of which we learn abruptly that he, too, will seek, not the Grail, but the lance, and that the land to which it brings woe is Logres, which should be not the Fisher's realm, but Arthur's. But Chrétien resumes Perceval, bringing him, after five years' wandering in which he forgets God, to a hermit, who proves to be his uncle. The Fisher is another uncle, and the Grail serves the Fisher's father. There is neither pike, lamprey, nor salmon in it, but a single Host, which has kept him alive. The hermit then teaches Perceval a prayer, only to be used in great peril.

Chrétien reverts to Gawain, and leaves the poem unfinished, without telling us any more of Perceval or the Grail. He has not even told what a Grail is. The name seems to be from the low Latin *cratalis*, and to signify a bowl or deep dish for serving food, rather than a cup.

Chrétien's fragment occupies about 10,000 lines. The next 24,000 lines are the most puzzling part of the poem. Some critics find here only a single hand, that of a certain Wauchier de Denain. He does not, however, name himself until near the end, after the narrative has at long last returned to Perceval. And the balance of opinion is in favour of assigning the earlier part, which is wholly Gawain matter, to another writer, called for convenience Pseudo-Wauchier. This is the part of the poem where the absence of a critical edition is most baffling. The divergence of the manuscripts suggests that it has, in any event, undergone a good deal of interpolation. But the nucleus seems to show a style distinct from that either of Chrétien or of Wauchier. They are court-poets—*trouvères*. Pseudo-Wauchier is a minstrel. His work is full of the minstrel's characteristic appeals to his audiences, and of references to a great 'conte' from which he claims to draw. Minstrelsy is, of course, an earlier literary development than court-poetry, which is for readers, not hearers. But one must not infer from this that Pseudo-Wauchier wrote before Chrétien and Wauchier. The minstrel did not at once disappear, even from courts, when the *trouvère* came. And in fact it is clear that, to some extent at least, Pseudo-Wauchier is merely a continuator of Chrétien. He begins by taking up a Gawain adventure which Chrétien left unfinished, and conducting it to a reasonable conclusion. Of this section some manuscripts give a shorter and some a longer form, and the longer describes a visit of Gawain to the Grail Castle. I shall not dwell on this, because it is probably an interpolation and a mere variant of the adventure to which we shall come in a moment. Then follow two long sections. Probably both are interpolations, and one certainly is; it is a romance of Caradoc, unconcerned with either Gawain, or Perceval, or the Grail. A string of new Gawain adventures then begins, and in one of these we reach the Grail again.

Gawain has rescued an unknown knight, and is taking him to Arthur's court, when a javelin from an unseen hand slays the knight. Gawain puts on the knight's armour, and rides in search of his name. He enters a chapel, where a Black Hand comes through the window and extinguishes the light on the altar. Gawain rides on, past the limits of Britain, and at nightfall reaches the sea. There is a long causeway, overhung by branches. The sea beats upon it. Gawain's horse takes the bit between his teeth, and carries him unwilling along this path. The traverse is very picturesquely described. At midnight they reach a great hall, full of folk, who greet Gawain with joy. But when they look in his face they say: ''Tis not he whom we

6

awaited', and leave the hall. Gawain looks round in anger. He beholds a bier, and on it a dead body, and on the body the fragment of a sword, broken below the hilt. While Gawain stands perplexed, a procession of canons enters, and the vigil of the dead is chanted. The hall is now filled with folk again, who make weeping and lamentation. Then those first seen by Gawain enter with cloths and napkins. There is a King, tall and strong of limb, not old but bald, fair and courteous. He bids Gawain sit. The Grail serves them. No hand holds it, but it comes and goes. Gawain knows not what to make of it. The King bids clear the hall and leaves Gawain alone. He sees a lance, fixed at the head of the daïs, with tapers before it. The blade is white as snow. It stands in a silver vessel, into which falls a stream of blood from the point. The King re-enters, bearing a sword. Weeping, he leads Gawain to the bier, and prays for revenge, 'so that the folk be once more joyful, and the land re-peopled, which by ye and this sword are wasted and made void'. He draws the sword; it is only a broken hilt. He bids Gawain join it to the fragment on the bier. Gawain tries, but in vain. The King leads him to another chamber, and tells him that he cannot achieve the quest, but may return. 'He who had undertaken the enterprise hath remained in your country. I know not what hath delayed him, but long have we awaited his coming.' Gawain may have what treasure he will, and may ask of the marvels. Gawain feels sleepy, but asks

7

of the lance, the sword, and the dead knight. The lance is that of Longinus, who pricked Christ on the cross. The sword struck the blow which brought destruction on Logres, and laid the country waste. The King will tell who the slayer and the slain were. He weeps. But Gawain has fallen asleep. In the morning he is on a rock by the sea, and near him are his horse and armour. No castle is visible. He resolves to return. As he rides, the land is rich with wood, water, and pastures. Yet it had been a waste land, and when Gawain asked of the lance, the waters flowed and the woods greened. 'So was the land in part re-peopled, but more might not be, since he had asked no more.' Folk meet him and bless him, and at the same time curse him for not asking of the Grail.

Pseudo-Wauchier turns to the adventures of Gawain's son. Presently Wauchier takes up the pen, and tells of Perceval. He is a poor writer, and has some very commonplace episodes. Once Perceval sees a light in the forest; it comes from the Grail, which the Fisher King carries with him to preserve him from mortal sin. And in the end he drifts back to the Grail Castle, entering on his way the Chapel of the Black Hand, where now a dead knight lies on the altar. The Fisher King is still on his couch. A damsel carries in the Grail and another the lance; a squire follows with a broken sword. Perceval asks, not of these, but of the dead knight. He is bidden to join the pieces of the sword; and does so, imperfectly, for a crack is left. The quest is not yet fully achieved, but the King embraces him, and hails him as lord of his house.

Wauchier now, in his turn, stops abruptly. I believe that he gives us nothing which is not based, with a minimum of invention, upon what Chrétien and Pseudo-Wauchier had already written; and that any reconstruction of the original conception of the Grail must rest upon Chrétien's Perceval visit and Pseudo-Wauchier's Gawain visit alone. The relation between these two is not so clear. How far do they agree? Wherein do they differ?

They have in common the Grail itself and the banquet which it serves (not quite explicitly in Chrétien); the lance; a sword; the castle by the water; the visiting stranger; the kingly host; the unasked question; its reaction on the well-being of the land; the disappearance of the castle in the morning. But the divergence is at least as remarkable as the agreement. In Chrétien the Grail and lance enter in procession. In Pseudo-Wauchier they are seen independently. Nobody carries the Grail; it moves by itself. The lance is fixed in the hall. There is nothing to suggest that the vessel into which the lance bleeds is identical with the Grail. The silver carving-dish of Chrétien's procession, perhaps not very significant, is not there. Pseudo-Wauchier's sword has to be joined as part of the quest; it seems to serve no purpose, at the castle itself, in Chrétien. Gawain's horse, not Perceval's, bears him to the castle against his will. Pseudo-Wauchier's King is robust, Chrétien's maimed.

9

He is a Fisher in Chrétien, not in Pseudo-Wauchier. Pseudo-Wauchier has no unseen old father, fed by the Grail. Chrétien has no dead knight wailed for on his bier. The evil state of the land is one of turbulence in Chrétien. In Pseudo-Wauchier it is definitely agricultural; the land has lost its fertility, and is waste.

What is the relation between the two accounts? Pseudo-Wauchier is certainly still to some extent continuing Chrétien. The expected visitor, who had tarried long, and for whom Gawain was at first taken, can only be Perceval. No doubt something of what Chrétien had written has been forgotten. Gawain must have heard of Perceval's adventure; was indeed present when the loathly lady came to upbraid Perceval. And in Chrétien he had vowed himself to seek the lance. He ought not, then, to see it with such surprise. But we need not be taken aback by such inconsistencies in a continuation.

The divergences, however, in the incidents at the castle itself can hardly be a matter of forgetfulness. And they seem too fundamental to be explained by a mere desire for artistic variation of detail. Moreover, although each writer has introduced elements both of chivalry and of Christianity, it is difficult for a reader of folk-tales to resist the conviction that these have been superimposed upon a story, which in its origin was neither Christian nor chivalric. And the folk-tale elements, the 'helpful' horse, the joining sword, and in particular the waste land, are certainly more obvious in Pseudo-Wauchier than in his predecessor. Did he bring these in from other stories known to him, or did he and Chrétien, directly or indirectly, use the same folk-tale as a source, and preserve different features from it? I incline to the latter solution.

I turn now to various interpretations which have been offered of the original motive. Alfred Nutt equated the Grail, lance, and sword with the talismans of the Celtic divinities, which appear in the *Second Battle of Moytura*, 'the ever-victorious spear of Lug, the irresistible sword of Nuada, and the never-failing caldron of the Dagda'. This analogy is not complete, because the *Moytura* story names a fourth talisman, the Inisfail or stone of knowledge —'He under whom it would cry out was King of Ireland'—and of this there is no trace in our Grail visits, unless it is buried under Chrétien's silver carving-dish. It should perhaps be added that in Wolfram von Eschenbach's *Parzival* the Grail itself is a stone, and has a power of election. No doubt there is a resemblance between the Grail and the caldron of the Dagda, which is only one of many vessels of abundance to be found, not only in Celtic legend, but in the folk-tales of divers peoples. They belong properly to the lords of the otherworld, from whom culture-heroes, such as Arthur, loot them. So far as the talismans play any active part in the *Battle of Moytura*, they help the gods to vanquish their adversaries. But we get no further towards understanding what was to happen at the Grail

Castle. There is no suggestion that Perceval or Gawain was to carry away the talismans, or that the lance was to be used in an impending battle.

A theory put forward by Miss Weston has received from folk-lorists a measure of acceptance which somewhat amazes me. There were certain agricultural fertility cults of the Eastern Mediterranean, in which the worshippers mimed the death and resurrection of a vegetation spirit. There were weeping and lamentation around the bier of an Adonis or an Attis, and joy at his uprising. These ceremonies secured the fertility of the crops and herds, and of the human race. Ultimately they became, in much altered forms, the basis of some of the various religions which competed with Christianity in the Roman world of the third and fourth centuries. These were personal religions, and their aim was not agricultural fertility, but philosophic contact with the divine, and in particular an assurance of immortality. But the believers were banded in gilds, and in their ritual and the initiation of their members they made symbolic use of the old agricultural practices. The prevailing spirit of syncretism affected Christianity itself, and there seems to have been a heretical sect, which identified Attis with its own divinity, and shared in his mysteries. These were closely linked with those of Mithraism, the most important of the non-Christian religions, and particularly affected by soldiers, who carried it all over the Roman world, even to the limits of Britain. Women were excluded from the

mysteries of Mithra, and for them the mysteries of
Attis served instead. Miss Weston assumes, without evidence, that these also reached Britain. And
she regards the Grail legend as the story of an
initiation into this cult, an initiation *manqué*, since
the failure to ask the required question barred
progress. It is to be noted that the theory implies
the unrecorded survival of the Attis cult in Britain
from the fourth century to the twelfth, since Miss
Weston supposes that Robert de Boron was familiar
with the original significance of the Grail. This is,
I think, frankly incredible. Nor does Miss Weston's
reminder that Mithraism lingered in the Alps and
Vosges to the fifth century go far to bridge a span
of eight hundred years. Equally unconvincing are
the detailed parallels which she arrays. There were
weeping and lamentation around the bier in the
Grail Castle. But other deaths have been mourned
besides that of Attis. The achievement of the quest
would have restored fertility to the land. But the
goal of the mysteries had long ceased to be agricultural fertility. Miss Weston finds sexual sym-
bols, such as the mysteries very likely used, in the
lance and the Grail. No doubt there are analogies
in many forms of nature worship. But I do not
think that there is anything of the kind in the Grail
story. A maiden carries the Grail, says Miss
Weston, and a youth the lance. It is so in Chrétien,
and it is not so in Pseudo-Wauchier, but surely it
has no significance. The lance bleeds into the Grail,
says Miss Weston. It does not in Chrétien. I do

not think that it does in Pseudo-Wauchier. It bleeds into a vessel, but that is not said to be the Grail. Then there is the unasked question. Certainly there were formulas to be learnt by the postulant in the mysteries, and things said, as well as things done, at the initiations. But we do not in fact know that the postulant was called on to ask a question. Finally, Miss Weston tells us that there are still correspondences to the Grail in the secret rituals of existing occult societies. It is very likely. But a secret oral tradition carries no proof of its origin or antiquity, and in fact the Grail legend was already extant in print and available as material for the syncretistic founders of Rosicrucianism in the sixteenth century. I reject Miss Weston *in toto*.

The views of Nutt and of Miss Weston are conflated in the recent book of Professor Loomis on *Celtic Myth and Arthurian Romance*. He thinks that the Celts had a fertility cult with initiation rites of their own, more like the original Eastern rites than the later philosophised mysteries, and possibly derived from the east through that western door of access from the Mediterranean, of which Sir Arthur Keith has lately written. Strabo told of an island near Britain where sacrifices were offered to Demeter and Kore, like those in Samothrace. A sexual vessel and spear in these came to be identified with those of Lug and the Dagda, and Professor Loomis conjectures that the end of the Grail story was a ritual marriage between the destined hero and the damsel who bore the Grail. I must repeat that the story as we have it attaches no significance to the lady. But Professor Loomis identifies her with Perceval's sister and his love Blancheflor, and with the many loves of Gawain, and with most of the female divinities in Celtic and Greek mythology. I really do not know what to make of Professor Loomis. He has written some valuable papers upon the iconography of the Arthur legends. But he seems to think that anything which anybody ever said about the Grail, down to *Arthur of Little Britain* and Sir Thomas Malory, can be used indifferently for the reconstruction of the original story. This seems to me to defy any reasonable theory as to the methods of mediæval writers and their relations to mythical or folk-lore sources. Of course, we know nothing of the details of any agricultural cults that may have developed on Celtic ground. Nor, in fact, do we know that the Grail story was of Celtic origin.

A different line is taken by Professor A. C. L. Brown. He regards the Grail story as a duplicate of that to which it is linked through Perceval, the rape of Arthur's cup by the Red Knight. Originally the older king at the Grail Castle was none other than the sleeping Arthur. Both stories are to be explained by the Irish *Battle of Moytura*. Here the gods are at war with giants, who have stolen their talismans, and thus enchanted the divine land. The destined hero, Lug or Perceval, recovers the talismans and is thus enabled to remove the enchantment. Unfortunately, Professor Brown has re-written all the stories before proceeding to explain them. Lug fights, in the *Battle of Moytura*, with an enchanted spear, but its relation to the four talis-mans of the Celtic gods is left quite uncertain. These are barely mentioned in the obscure narratives of the *Battle* which have reached us. They seem to remain inert, and certainly are not said to have been stolen by the giants. Nor is there anything to show that the cup taken from Arthur's table was a talisman. As we hear of it, it is an ordinary cup. That Arthur was in woe at the insult, and cheered up when the cup was recovered, is really not, as Professor Brown thinks, proof of its magical qualities. The insult is purely chivalric. Nor does anyone steal the Grail. There are stories of Finn, in which a demon comes through a window and troubles a feast. Professor Brown is reduced to the conjecture that this once happened at the Grail Castle, and that the incident has been transferred to the Chapel of the Black Hand, which Gawain passes on the way thither. This is surely a master-piece of perversion.

I find all these theories unsatisfactory. It is only with diffidence that I sketch another. The early history of the Priest-Kingship forms a large part of the subject of Frazer's *Golden Bough*. He traces it to the human representative of the vegetation spirit, imbued with its fertilising power, and an-nually slain and replaced by a successor for the renewal of that power. But of course Kingship went through many stages. The victim became a medicine-man, securing fertility by means of magic rites and implements. He was not content to die at the end of a year, and prolonged his reign. But the energy of natural production was still bound up with his vitality, and when that failed he must at last die and a successor be found. This stage is still represented by the Shilluk tribe of the White Nile.

The King, though regarded with reverence, must not be allowed to become old or feeble, lest, with the diminishing vigour of the ruler, the cattle should sicken and fail to bear increase, the crops should rot in the field, and men die in ever-growing numbers. One of the signs of failing energy is the King's inability to fulfil the desires of his wives, of whom he has a large number. When this occurs the wives report the fact to the chiefs, who condemn the King to death forthwith, communicating the sentence to him by spreading a white cloth over his face and knees during his mid-day slumber. Formerly the King was starved to death in a hut, in company with a young maiden. It is believed that he is now strangled.[1]

And how is a royal successor appointed? Ultimately, of course, through heredity, either in the male or female line. The medicine-man has established not only himself but his dynasty. Often again by election, among the members of the royal family, among the chiefs, or among all comers. The choice may rest with the women of the harem. That

[1] I adapt the summary in J. L. Weston, *From Ritual to Romance*, 56.

is fortuitous enough. But there are more fortuitous methods still. The candidates may compete in battle, in a race, even in answering riddles. They do that in *Pericles*. Often again there is some method of divination. Of this there are many traces in folk-tales, of which a large collection may be found in a paper by Dr Hartland on *The Voice of the Stone of Destiny*.[1] The divination may be by dream or omen. In Persia, according to Herodotus, the chief whose horse neighed first was chosen. It may be by accident; the first stranger at the gate is taken. But often there is some more symbolical sign of divine will, if one likes to put it so. In legends of papal elections, a candidate's taper bursts into flame, or a bell rings when he passes under it, or a dove descends on his head. These are Christianised in sentiment, but they echo the folk-tales. In many of the latter the agent of the divination is something connected with the former King. Here, too, a royal bird descends. The royal horses go unguided to a house. The royal elephant kneels before a man, or lifts him on to its back, or puts a garland round his neck. And finally the choice may rest not with the royal animals or birds, but with the royal insignia. The crown floats through the air to a head. The chariot bearing the sword, parasol, fan, diadem, and slippers stops. The jewelled shoes fit, the throne remains steadfast, the diadem unshaken. The Inisfail, as we have seen, roars. And what are the insignia but the wonder-working

[1] *Folk-Lore*, xiv, 28.

instruments of the medicine-man, become talismans? Is it not possible that the Grail story was
originally one of the choice of a successor by the
royal talismans themselves? The broken sword of
royalty is pieced at his touch; that fits well enough.
And to the question, 'Who is served by the Grail?'
may not the answer, in some symbolic form, have
been, 'We serve thee, O King'. Perhaps the spear
of victory, which was dry, began to bleed again,
and the vessel of abundance, which was empty, was
refilled. And the land, which was waste through
the lost virility of the old King, smitten like the King
of the Shilluk in his organs of increase, gives of its
fruits once more. Of course, the romancers have
altered much. The Grail King has somehow been
duplicated. The testing was to have been spread
out over a succession of visits. Chrétien, in particular, has obscured the purpose of the sword, and
probably contemplated some Christianisation of
the Grail and lance as Holy Blood relics. One does
not know how he would have worked it out. And
he has made Perceval a kinsman of the Grail house.
But that is common in the folk-tales themselves.
They have passed through minds familiar with the
principle of heredity. It is often not the kingdom
which the stranger wins, but the hand of the King's
daughter. Divination confirms rather than confers
a claim. I doubt whether there is any significance
in the fishing. The tale may originally have been told
of a fisher-folk. We do not know where it comes
from. Pseudo-Wauchier seems to refer to himself

as a man of Lothian. Nor do we know whether it attached itself first to Perceval or to Gawain. Stories of Gawain seem to have hung about the north of Britain. But probably it was originally anonymous. The Fisher King is given no personal name in the *Conte del Graal*.

# SIR THOMAS MALORY

SIR THOMAS MALORY came late to his high theme. The heyday of Arthurian romance was over by the middle of the thirteenth century. Then began the period of scribes and interpolators, with their sequels and *enfances*. The outlines of the old stories were blurred, their movement slowed down under the accumulation of subsidiary adventures, conventional and interminable. They had always been long-winded enough; the evenings in a mediæval castle, when the day's fighting was over, were long. The alliterative revival of the fourteenth century gave some fresh impulse, but it passed. Then the *Romance of the Rose* brought in a new mode of sentimental allegory, and Chaucer followed with his quicker and more vivid way of telling tales. Moreover, the best of the romances were still in French, and cultivated England was ceasing to talk French. They became old-fashioned, and at the most contributed to balladry. It is the popular literature—ballads, carols, miracle-plays— which counts most in the fifteenth century; except for Malory himself, who has nothing to do with all these. And so when Malory began to turn over the faded manuscripts in the window-seat of some country manor, and to shape them into his strong new prose, he was almost as deliberate an archaist as the writer of *The Faerie Queene* or the writer of *The Defence of Guenevere*. It was not all loss.

Detached from the tradition, he had to pour some new wine into the old bottles, to bring his antiquarian findings into some kind of vital relation to the thought and conditions of his own day. I shall come back to that.

Just now I want to remind you how difficult Malory's material was to handle, and to note some weak points in his handling. I am not going to linger over this; it is an intricate subject, for which all the evidence is not yet available, while some of what is available has not always been wisely used.[1] But I think it is clear that the process of 'reducing' out of French into English, of which Caxton's preface to the *Morte d'Arthur* speaks, must have involved not merely the work of an abbreviator and translator, but also a good deal of selection and compilation from different sources. There is no trace of any single French book which remotely resembles Malory's. He must have had several manuscripts at his disposal, perhaps more than one would expect to find kept together, anywhere outside some great household. A few of them contained versions of tales other than those contained in the manuscripts we know, or tales not otherwise known at all. But as a rule we can determine the kind of manuscript he used. He must have had the comprehensive romance of *Lancelot*, of which there are five sections, the Early History of the Grail, the Merlin, the Lancelot proper, the Quest of the Grail, and the Mort Artus. This was itself to some

[1] See now E. Vinaver, *Malory* (1929).

extent of composite origin, although the latest investigation, that of M. Ferdinand Lot, tends to ascribe four of the five sections to a single hand, and to regard only the Merlin as an interpolation. He had the other vast romance of *Tristan*, in a late and debased form. He had, perhaps unfortunately, a variant of the Merlin, written to lead up to a version of the Quest of the Grail, other than that given in the *Lancelot*. And, Caxton notwithstanding, he had English sources, as well as French; the alliterative *Morte d'Arthur*, upon which he based his account of Arthur's wars with Rome, and perhaps the fourteenth-century metrical *Morte d'Arthur*, which shares many of Malory's divergences from the *Lancelot* in the last stages of his story. I have said enough to show that the material was complex. The bulk alone was very great; ten times that of the *Morte d'Arthur*. Some of the adventures told were essential to the working out of the main themes; others were incidental, and led nowhere. There was an obvious danger, in a drastic reduction, of taking the incidental and missing the essential. Moreover, the romances had slowly grown into their latest forms. They had influenced and counter-influenced each other in diverse fashions. They had heroes and adventures in common, but the adventures did not always work out in the same way, and the heroes did not always sustain the same characters. Sir Thomas Malory had not, even to the extent to which we have, the clue of scholarship to enable him to thread these mazes. With all deference to a really great writer, I think that, so far as the first half of the *Morte d'Arthur* is concerned, he rather bungled his structural problem. We expect a work of fiction to have a beginning, a middle, and an end; to progress, however deviously, through the medium of consistent personalities, to an intelligible issue. The *Morte d'Arthur* does not satisfy this expectation. That is why, through so much of it, we walk perplexedly. It is, in the phrase of a poet of our own day, 'the dim Arthuriad'. It is full of beginnings which have no end and of ends which never had a beginning. It does not perhaps matter much that knights who have been killed in one book live to fight and be killed again in another. But Merlin comes and goes, and we are never told who or what Merlin is. First Pellinore and then Palamydes pursues the questing beast, but the nature of the quest remains dark. The adventures of Balin bear many suggestions of their significance in relation to the Grail, but when the book of the Grail comes, they are found not to have been significant. Malory has in his hands two of the world's dozen great love stories, and does not succeed in telling either of them completely. The earlier scenes between Tristram and Iseult are hidden in an overgrowth of commonplace chivalric adventures, the chief purposes of which are to pit Tristram against Lancelot, to let Iseult write sentimental letters to Guenevere, and to make King Mark quite unnecessarily contemptible. And then we are told, 'Here endeth the

24

second book of Sir Tristram. But here is no re-
hearsal of the third book'. And so we are left to
hear of Tristram's death by a casual report in a
later book, and then it is not the pathetic and
imaginative story of the black sail, with which we
are familiar from the old poems, but only a
treacherous stabbing in the back by Mark. It is
not altogether Malory's fault. He did not know
the old poems, and the prose *Tristan* was the worst
of models. Perhaps he would have done better
to have left the *Tristan* alone, and kept to the
*Lancelot*. But if he robs us of the end of Tristram,
he robs us of the beginning of Lancelot. There is
nothing of the changeling boyhood, nothing of the
coming to court and of Lancelot's trembling at the
sight of Guenevere; not even that episode of the
first kiss, of which Dante makes such unforgettable
use in the *Divine Comedy*. The outcome of Lancelot's relation with Guenevere, as we shall see, is
nobly treated; but the relation itself is taken for
granted, and is not led up to. It therefore, to some
extent, fails to carry us with it. One point more,
and I shall be glad to have done with depreciation.
A solution of continuity which affects character is
more serious than one which merely affects plot.
And one important character at least, that of
Gawain, is not maintained on the same plane
throughout. In all the earlier Arthurian romances
Gawain is the noblest of Arthur's knights; he is
'Gawane the gay, gratious, and gude', the em-
bodiment of courtesy, always contrasted with Kay

25

the churlish and crabbed. Then somebody, Walter Map or another, invented Lancelot, and made him the queen's lover, and the imagination of the romance writers took hold of Lancelot and he became the leading knight of the Round Table, ousting Gawain. But for the purposes of the Lancelot romance Gawain, although relegated to the second place, must remain noble, and Lancelot's true comrade in arms, until some inevitable break comes, which dissolves the high companionship, and precipitates the ultimate tragedy of the Mort Artus. And so it is in Malory's opening and closing books. But so it is not throughout the story. I do not merely mean that Gawain, as a worldly man and a lover of light ladies, is not thought worthy to achieve the Holy Grail, and, to say the truth, does not much mind whether he achieves it or not. Lancelot himself does not achieve the Holy Grail. But in the Tristram section there is a systematic blackening of Gawain's character as a knight. He slays the good Sir Lamorak by treachery, and we are told that privily he hated Sir Lancelot and all his kin, and that 'after Sir Gareth had espied Sir Gawain's conditions, he withdrew himself from his brother Sir Gawain's fellowship, for he was vengeable, and where he hated he would be avenged with murder, and that hated Sir Gareth'. Malory has forgotten this, when he comes to the Mort Artus, but the reader cannot forget.

What then should be the attitude of criticism in

the face of all this structural incoherence? One way is to demonstrate that Malory is much more subtle than we took him for, and that, when he seems most artless, he is really laying the threads of his deliberate design. This is the way adopted in a recent book on the *Morte d'Arthur* which reached me as I was meditating these observations. The other is to accept the facts, and to take Malory for what he can give, and not for what he cannot give. That is, I think, the better way. There are stirring and amusing tales enough in the earlier books, even if they are episodic and do not advance a main theme; the tale of Arthur's fight with the giant on St Michel, for example, or that of Gareth's adventures with the minx Lynette. Or you may regard the whole thing as a tapestry; half close your eyes and watch a pleasant landscape, full of running waters, and moated castles, and hermitages, and green lawns, and 'plumps' of wood, among which move bright little figures in blue and white and red armour, every now and again stopping to lay spears in rest and upset one another, and then swearing eternal friendship and riding away again. Here is a ford perilous, and at the door of a pavilion a dwarf watches a shield, hung there for the challenge of any knight who has a mind to end an ill custom. There a tired knight sleeps under a great apple-tree that stands by a hedge, and presently his horse grimly neighs, and by sweep four queens on white mules under a canopy of green silk, and cast an enchantment upon him. They are Morgan le Fay

27

and her sisters, high-born dames, but 'nigro-
mancers' all. And presently knights and ladies
begin to gather from their several adventures, and
turn their horses' heads all one way. They are
making for the great tournament beside Lonazep.
The name sounds full of promise. But it is not
worth while following them; the great tournament
beside Lonazep is a tournament like any other. And
throughout you have the delight of Malory's ad-
mirable prose; as finished an instrument in its way
as any prose the sixteenth century can show, but
with the freshness of the early world still upon it.
A formal analysis of style would be tedious. I
choose three points only for illustration. The first
is the constant use of vivid words, which have now
gone out of the language. A knight rides 'a great
wallop' until he comes to a fountain. Another is
smitten on a ship and falls down 'noseling' to
the shipboard. Lancelot tilts with Gawain and
charges him 'so sore that his horse reversed up so
down'. A tall lad is a 'much young man'. Arthur
has a dream of a fight in the air between a boar and
a dragon, in which 'the dragon flew away all on a
height, and come down with such a swough, and
smote the boar to powder, both flesh and bones,
that it fluttered all abroad on the sea'. Sometimes
there is an echo of the alliterative poems. Gawain
comes to battle 'as brim as any boar'. Bedivere
sees 'the waters wap and waves wan'. Such phrases
are racy of the vernacular, but it is French, although
it sounds like English, when Gawain bids Lancelot

28

'deliver the queen from thee and pike thee lightly out of the court'. It is both French and English, when Sir Bors sees 'a spear great and long that came straight upon him pointling'. The tempers of the two languages are coalescing. So much for my first stylistic point. The second is that, although there is little word-painting, Malory is alive to the sweet influences of the Pleiades. His adventures are hung about, like English sport, with outdoor sights and sounds. Knights ride to keep their tryst, and 'lodge them in a little leaved wood, beside there the tournament should be'. They fight with such dint of strokes 'that the noise and sound rang by the water and the wood'. A fight lasts all day, and at evensong 'they set them down upon two mole-hills there beside the fighting place, and either of them unlaced his helm and took the cold wind'. A tired man comes to a fair well and puts off his helm 'to drink of that burbley water'. Another is caught in a storm, when there fell 'a thunder and a rain, as heaven and earth should go together'. More elaborate is the picture when Arthur meets a churl at the door of his castle in Sherwood. 'He was all befurred in black sheepskins, and a great pair of boots, and a bow and arrows, in a russet gown, and brought wild geese in his hand, and it was on the morn after Candlemas day.' It is Merlin in disguise, coming across the snows of Candlemas. My third point is a trick of dialogue. Malory can be rhetorical, when a dramatic need calls for it. But for the most part the knights are of brief speech. They are men of their hands. Arthur has to face the challenge of six kings at once, and asks advice of his barons. 'They could no counsel give, but said they were big enough.' Could a war debate among English lords be better or more briefly rendered? But a wind-bag will get his answer. 'As for that threatening, said Sir Gringamore, be it as it may, we will go to dinner.' And when Turquine has flung his defiance at the whole of the Table Round, 'That is over much said, said Sir Lancelot'. The phrasing may shape itself in gnomic homespun. 'What, nephew, said the king, is the wind in that door?' When Lancelot's time of trouble comes, his fellowship recall that they have had much weal with him and much worship. 'And therefore, Sir Lancelot, said they, we will take the woe with the weal.' These brevities of speech are Malory's nearest approach to humour. Fundamental humour, the humour of a Chaucer, is perhaps incompatible with romance. It shatters the dome of many-coloured glass. Chaucer and Shakespeare between them did not leave much romance about Troilus and Cressida.

Towards the middle of the *Morte d'Arthur*, light breaks over the story. We no longer see men walking as trees darkly. They begin to arrange themselves in definite patterns, and to move through real conflicts of character and passion to a deliberate end. Henceforward everything centres round Lancelot; we get clear of the *Tristan*. Malory is ruthless in abridging his source, taking only so

30

much from the intricate adventures of the French
*Lancelot* as will establish, firstly, his hero's priority
to all the other knights of the Round Table,
secondly, the special link between him and Gawain
and his brother Gareth, thirdly, his love relation
with Guenevere, and, fourthly, his parentage of
Galahad. Lancelot may not himself see the Grail,
but he cannot, in a Lancelot romance, give place to
any of his fellows. So the Grail-winner must be
his son, and as Lancelot will love no woman but
Guenevere, the existence of a son must be explained
by bringing Lancelot under a spell. Spells are
always legitimate in romance. Galahad is born,
grows up, comes to court, and achieves the siege
perilous. And so the story slides into the Quest of
the Grail. I hope I shall not imperil sympathy if
I say that I do not regard the Quest of the Grail as
one of the most satisfactory parts of the *Morte
d'Arthur*. Again it is not altogether Malory's fault.
He follows the French *Lancelot* closely here, and
the Quest, as he tells it, was an integral part of the
*Lancelot*, perhaps from the beginning, and certainly
in the version which came down to him and has
come to us. But the much-told tale is told better
elsewhere. The Galahad Quest has not the mystery
of Chrétien de Troyes' original fragment; it may be
just because it is not a fragment. It has not the
tender melancholy of the *Perlesvaus*, the version
translated as *The High History of the Holy Grail*.
German scholars find a deeper humanity in Wolfram von Eschenbach's *Parzival*. The introduction

31

of the theme into the *Lancelot* explains itself well enough. It is a quite legitimate attempt to bring romance into the service of religious mysticism. It points from the way of earthly achievement to the way of spiritual illumination. The chivalry of heaven is set against the chivalry of the Round Table. But the initial inspiration, whatever its worth, is insufficient to carry the writer through his long series of symbolic adventures and still more symbolic visions, with a hermit waiting at every crossroads to expound the symbolism in its bitterest detail. The hermit had ill success with the frivolous Gawain. 'Sir, said Sir Gawain, and I had leisure I would speak with you, but my fellow here, Sir Ector, is gone, and abideth me yonder beneath the hill. Well, said the good man, thou were better to be counselled.' Do not our hearts, in these long books, sometimes go down the hill with Gawain? Structurally, too, the Quest makes a false issue in the story. When Galahad comes to court with his unearthly beauty, and all the knights turn to their new avows, Arthur is 'displeased'. He foresees the end of the Table Round.

For when they depart from hence, I am sure they all shall never meet more in this world, for they shall die many in the quest. And so it forthinketh me a little, for I have loved them as well as my life, wherefore it shall grieve me right sore the departition of this fellowship, for I have had an old custom to have them in my fellowship. And there with the tears fill in his eyne.

32

The Round Table had worked for the betterment of human life, but of this, as the history of religious thought has shown, the mystic impulse may take hardly more account than of 'the vain glory of the world, the which is not worth a pear'. But if a theme of mysticism were to be the issue of Malory's story, surely it should have ended with this theme. It ends quite differently. The Grail vanishes. The knights who achieve it are those who have least to do with the Round Table. The old motives of life re-establish themselves. Only in Lancelot is a little sting of conscience left; he has been of the Quest, and has failed. And the ultimate debate, upon which the fortunes of Arthur and his fellowship break and are dissolved, is not between the ideals of Camelot and the ideals of Corbenic, but a purely human one, the familiar conflict between human love and human loyalty.

The two books which follow the Quest contain four great adventures of Lancelot. Three of them concern his relations with Guenevere; his services to her in the delivery from the stake and the rescue from Sir Meliagrance; his renunciation for her in the beautiful tale of the fair maid of Astolat. The epilogue hints at the problem which is coming.

For, Madam, said Sir Lancelot, I love not to be constrained to love; for love must arise of the heart, and not by no constraint. That is truth, said the king, and many knights: love is free in himself, and never will be bounden; for where he is bounden he loseth himself.

33

There is already tragic irony here. The fourth adventure shows Lancelot at the top of his knightly renown. He alone, of all the Round Table, may touch Sir Urre's wounds and heal them. And when the adventure is over, 'ever Sir Lancelot wept as he had been a child that had been beaten'. That is a fine touch of Malory's. The περιπέτεια, the tragic reversal of fortunes, is upon us. And now, with the last two books, Malory rises to the full height of his epic theme. May I call it epic? Professor Ker, to whom in all things mediæval we are bound to defer, draws a sharp distinction between epic and romance, between Roland or Beowulf and Lancelot. For him the epic is the heroic. The defence of a narrow place against odds, dramatically told; that is a typical heroic or epic adventure. Well, I do not wish to deny the difference in temper between the *Chanson de Roland* and the *Lancelot*, with a century or more of romance-writing between them; although Lancelot was in a tight place enough when he slew Sir Colgrevaunce at the door of Guenevere's chamber, unarmed against fourteen knights who 'had gotten a great form out of the hall, and therewith they rashed at the door'. But common usage, I think, allows of many different tempers and manners of writing within the notion of epic, insisting only on dignity and scope of treatment, and on the linking up of individual fortunes with those of some greater whole, a house, a nation, an empire, humanity itself. This linking up does not fail in the *Morte d'Arthur*. Professor

Ker does not admit that the national or 'ecumenical' theme is of the essence of epic; he finds this rather in 'dramatic representation of the characters'. And he quotes Aristotle—always an excellent thing to do. Aristotle praises Homer because, while other poets 'tell their story straight on', he 'with little prelude, leaves the stage to personages, men and women, all with characters of their own'. It is true. But Aristotle is here contrasting the manner of a good epic poet with the manner of some bad epic poets. He is not trying to define the notion of epic. He does not say whether its theme should or should not have a national or ecumenical aspect. Certainly the *Iliad* is the tale of Troy, as well as the tale of the wrath of Achilles, and the *Odyssey* is not unconcerned with the dynasty of Ithaca. However this may be, Aristotle ought to have approved of the last two books of the *Morte d'Arthur*. Malory follows his precept exactly. There is a little prelude, and then, with rare comments, Malory stands aside and lets his characters speak and act for themselves. Here is the little prelude.

In May, when every lusty heart flourisheth and bourgeoneth; for as the season is lusty to behold and comfortable, so man and woman rejoicen and gladden of summer coming with his fresh flowers, for winter, with his rough winds and blasts, causeth a lusty man and woman to cower and sit fast by the fire. So in this season, as in the month of May, it befell a great anger and unhap that stinted not till the flower of chivalry of all the world was destroyed and slain; and all was long upon two unhappy knights, the which were named Agravaine and Sir Mordred that were brethren unto Sir Gawain.

The stage is now set. The action is swift, the conclusion inevitable; there is a full sense of the pity of it. The web of the psychological situation is closely woven. It is not merely the 'eternal triangle'; Lancelot, Arthur, Guenevere. Lancelot is the midmost figure, drawn this way by fidelity to his king, and that way by fidelity to his mistress. But there is also Mordred, the child of Arthur's sin, and destined from birth to be Arthur's undoing, working now actively with Agravaine for Lancelot's overthrow. And there are Gawain and Gareth, bound to Lancelot by all knightly bonds. He has rescued Gawain from Carados and Turquine; he has knighted Gareth and loves him. When the crisis comes, Gawain is for long true to Lancelot. Then, in rescuing Guenevere for the second time from the stake, Lancelot unwittingly slays the unarmed Gareth, and Gawain's love is turned to hate. His fiercer spirit compels the reluctant king to besiege the lovers in Joyous Gard. At this siege Lancelot's behaviour is perfect in its sad deference to an ancient loyalty. It is long before he will level a spear, and when Bors unhorses Arthur, Lancelot alights and horses him again, and 'the tears brast out of Arthur's eyes, thinking on the great courtesy that was in Sir Launcelot, more than in any other man'. The Pope intervenes and bids Arthur take his queen again and 'accord'

36

with Lancelot. Arthur consents. Lancelot rides
with the queen from Joyous Gard, which hereafter
shall be Dolorous Gard, to Carlisle, both clothed
alike in white cloth of gold tissue, with a hundred
knights in green velvet, and every knight 'with a
branch of olive in his hand in tokening of peace'.
It is his last pageant. He perjures himself, as
others in like case have done, and will do again.
Guenevere's reputation is to be unstained. And
now you think that her adventures at least are
ended, and that she will live it out at Carlisle or
Camelot, like that Helen whom Telemachus be-
held at Sparta, when Troy fires had long been dust,
τανύπεπλον, a comely housewife with her distaff
among her handmaidens. The story will have it
otherwise; but now it goes with Lancelot. Arthur
may be reconciled, but Gawain will not be reconciled. Lancelot must 'pike' him out of that court,
of which he had been at once the stay and ornament. Arthur and Gawain and their host follow
him over the seas to Benwick, and there, stung by
Gawain's insults, Lancelot twice lays him low,
and twice refuses to take his life. Then Mordred
strikes again, raising rebellion in Arthur's absence,
and claiming to wed Guenevere. Arthur returns.
Gawain dies of his old wound at Dover, and
relents, but all too late, bidding Arthur send for
Lancelot, and begging that Lancelot will visit his
tomb. The rest is familiar; the death of Arthur, the
pathetic farewell between Lancelot and Guenevere,
their edifying ends in their several hermitages,

37

Lancelot's burial at Joyous Gard, and Ector's threnody over his bier. No doubt it is in all the anthologies, but I cannot forbear to quote it.

Ah Launcelot, he said, thou were head of all Christian knights; and now I dare say, said Sir Ector, thou Sir Lancelot, there thou liest, that thou were never matched of earthly knight's hand; and thou were the courteoust knight that ever bare shield; and thou were the truest friend to thy lover that ever bestrad horse; and thou were the truest lover of a sinful man that ever loved woman; and thou were the kindest man that ever strake with sword; and thou were the goodliest person that ever came among press of knights; and thou was the meekest man and the gentlest that ever ate in hall among ladies; and thou were the sternest knight to thy mortal foe that ever put spear in the rest.

Such is Malory's music and such his meaning; and now he has nothing to do but to date his book, and bid his readers 'pray for me while I am on live that God send me good deliverance, and when I am dead, I pray you all pray for my soul'. What does he mean by 'good deliverance'? Until recently, little has been known of Malory's personality. Of himself he only tells us that he finished his work in 1469 or 1470, and that he was a knight, which has not prevented perverse commentators from arguing that he was a priest. But the research of Professor Kittredge has reasonably identified him with a certain Sir Thomas Malory of Newbold Revel in Warwickshire, who served in the train of that last paladin of chivalry, Richard Beauchamp, Earl of Warwick, and, if he did not himself see Agincourt, must at any rate have spent his youth in the atmosphere of national unity and military enterprise, of which the name of Agincourt remains the symbol. In later life he became a knight of the shire for Warwickshire, and it is probable that he was also the Thomas Malory, knight, who was excluded with others from two pardons of Edward IV, in 1468. If so, the 'deliverance' for which Malory prayed in 1469 or 1470 was deliverance from prison. I hope he got it. Probably he did. I do not think it should be inferred that Malory was a Lancastrian. A Warwickshire man is likely to have been a follower of Warwick the 'king-maker'. But the 'king-maker' was behind the disaffections of 1468. In 1469 he was at open war with Edward, and if Malory did not benefit by the amnesty of that year, he can hardly have remained a prisoner during the brief 're-adeption' of Henry VI, which began on October 9, 1470. A few days before it ended Malory died, on March 14, 1471. 'Valens miles' was on the tomb in the London Greyfriars, where he lay until the Reformation scattered his ashes. The direct echoes of his life in his book are not many. As I have said, like Homer, he rarely intervenes. But even as blind Homer introduces the blind Demodocus, so Malory, when he has described how Tristram fell into prison, passes to a comment:

So Sir Tristram endured there great pain, for sickness had undertaken him, and that is the greatest pain a prisoner may have. For all the while a prisoner may have his health of body, he may endure under the mercy of God, and in hope

39

of good deliverance; but when sickness touches a prisoner's body, then may a prisoner say all wealth is him bereft, and then he hath cause to wail and to weep.

This is one of three or four reflective passages which, so far as we can tell, Malory did not find in his sources. The most famous is the chapter on 'How true love is likened to summer', which introduces the tale of Guenevere's Maying. Some blossoming bough has flung itself across the window of his prison, and the old knight stops to muse on spring and love. This, too, is in all the anthologies. Another, and perhaps critically the most significant, is in the account of Mordred's rebellion, when the people were 'so new fangle' that for the most part they held with him.

Lo ye all Englishmen, see ye not what a mischief here was, for he that was the most king and knight of the world, and most loved the fellowship of noble knights, and by him they were all upholden, now might not these Englishmen hold them content with him. Lo thus was the old custom and usage of this land. And also men say that we of this land have not yet lost ne forgotten that custom and usage. Alas this is a great default of us Englishmen; for there may no thing please us no term.

Here then Malory reads a lesson. And indeed to regard the *Morte d'Arthur* as no more than a piece of archaistic romancing would be to mistake its temper. After all, Malory is writing with his eye on the fifteenth century. The Wars of the Roses were no crusade. Chivalry was not much in evidence when Lord Clifford stabbed young Rut-

land at the bridge of Wakefield. Lancelot would
not have done that. And so Malory, who remem-
bers Agincourt, will set before his countrymen the
ideal of a better England, an ideal in which the
knights are charged

never to do outrageousity, nor murder, and always to flee
treason. Also, by no mean to be cruel, but to give mercy
unto him that asketh mercy...; and always to do ladies,
damsels, and gentlewomen succour upon pain of death.
Also, that no man take no battles in a wrongful quarrel for
no law, ne for no world's goods. Unto this were all the
knights sworn of the Table Round, both old and young.

Can he bring back the days of King Arthur—or is
it the days of King Henry V?

Certainly the *Morte d'Arthur* is a book that makes
for righteousness. It was a singular aberration of
criticism when Roger Ascham wrote of it that 'the
whole pleasure standeth in two speciall poyntes, in
open mans slaughter and bold bawdry: in which
book these be counted the noblest knights, that do
kill most men without any quarrel, and commit
foulest adulteries by subtlest shifts'. I do not
claim that Malory sees his way quite clearly through
the queer spiritual tangle of the twelfth-century
*amour courtois*. Perhaps such casuistry was not for
him. He knows that love is good, and therefore of
Guenevere he will 'make here a little mention, that
while she lived she was a true lover, and therefore
she had a good end'. But he knows also that sin
brings tragedy. It is not merely that the sinful man
will not see the Holy Grail. The tragedy is here and

now. 'For as well as I have loved thee', says Guenevere to Lancelot, 'For as well as I have loved thee, mine heart will not serve me to see thee; for through thee and me is the flower of kings and knights destroyed.' Better than by Ascham, the spirit of the book is held by William Caxton, who, after the 'simple cunning' which God hath sent to him, will put it into print for an 'ensample'.

For herein may be seen noble chivalry, courtesy, humanity, friendliness, hardiness, love, friendship, cowardice, murder, hate, virtue and sin. Do after the good and leave the evil, and it shall bring you to good fame and renommee.

I sometimes wonder what democracy, with its transmutation of all literary as well as all social values, which is before us, will make of the *Morte d'Arthur*. Malory's is a very aristocratic ideal. The churl does not count for much in it. Agincourt was all very well, but I dare say Malory sat holding his spear at the siege of Rouen, when the townsfolk, after living on 'cattis, hors, houndis, rattis, myse, and all that myght be etynne', were driven out of the gates by the garrison 'for spendyng of vitaille', and remorselessly driven back into the moat by Henry's forces. I hope that he was one of the knights told off to take them a Christmas dinner there. In the *Morte d'Arthur* itself, the distinction between noble and churl is fundamental. If there are sparks of nobility in a cowherd's son, like Tor, or a kitchen knave, like Gareth, you may be sure he will turn out to be a king's son in disguise. There is much emphasis on lineage. That Lancelot and his son are 'the greatest gentlemen in the world' is quaintly explained. They are of the lineage of Jesus Christ. Percival and his brother may not dwell at home, 'for we be come of king's blood of both parties, and therefore, mother, it is our kind to haunt arms and noble deeds'. Even the hermits in Logres are of gentle birth.

> For in these days it was not the guise of hermits as is nowadays. For there were none hermits in those days, but that they had been men of worship and of prowess, and those hermits held great household, and refreshed people that were in distress.

Malory goes out of his way to give this bit of antiquarian lore. He must have known anchorites in his own time, whose salad even a wandering knight would not want to share. Well, when democracy comes to its own, I suppose that Lancelot will have to go through the crucible, with Plato's wardens and Aristotle's magnanimous man. And yet, after all, the transmutation of values is not the extinction of values. An economic redistribution will not wholly remove the need for chivalry. Even in the New Jerusalem, I think, there will be courtesies to be exchanged, wrongs to be righted, public service to be done. And so, perhaps, the lamps that burnt for our fathers may still glimmer upon our path, and it may still prove true that 'in him that should say or think that there was never a king called Arthur, might well be aretted great folly and blindness'.

43

# Sir Thomas Malory

## NOTE

Professor Kittredge's investigation of Malory's life is in a paper on *Who Was Sir Thomas Malory?* (1896, *Harvard Studies and Notes in Philology and Literature*, v, 85) and a shorter contribution to W. E. Mead, *Selections from Morte d'Arthur* (1897), xiv. One correction of fact and two or three additions, from sources not accessible when Professor Kittredge wrote, are desirable. Professor Kittredge, following Dugdale, gives the date of Malory's death as 1470. But this represents 1471 in our reckoning, which begins the year from January 1, not March 25. The original record, printed from Cotton MS. Vitellius F. xii in C. L. Kingsford, *The Grey Friars of London* (1915, *British Soc. of Franciscan Studies*), 93, runs 'In Capella Sancti Francisci...sub 2ª parte fenestre 4ᵉ sub lapide iacet dominus Thomas Mallere, valens miles: qui obiit 14 die mensis Marcij, Aᵒ dⁿˡ 1470, de parochia de Monkenkyrkby in comitatu Warwici'. Monks Kirby is near Newbold Revel, and the Malory arms were once in its church window. Here, too, was a priory once a cell of the monastery of St Nicholas of Angiers. On the suppression of the alien priories under Richard II, it was transferred to the Carthusian house of Epworth in the isle of Axholme, Lincolnshire. Henry IV restored it to Angiers, and Henry V in 1415–16 to Epworth again. The last transfer was confirmed by Edward IV in 1468–9. Some dispute as to this priory probably lies behind two commissions of Henry VI in which Malory figures (*Calendar of Patent Rolls, Hen. VI*, v, 476; vi, 61). The first, of July 13, 1451, directs Humphrey Duke of Buckingham and Richard Earl of Warwick to arrest Thomas Malory, knight, and his servant John Appelby, and cause them to find mainpernors who will mainprise for them under a sufficient penalty that they will do no hurt to the prior and convent of the Carthusian house of Axiholme or any of the king's people, and that they will appear in person before the king and council on the quinzaine of Michaelmas next to answer certain charges. The second, of March 26, 1452, directs the Duke of Buckingham, Sir Edward Grey of Groby, and the Sheriff of Warwick and Leicester to arrest 'Thomas Malorre, knight', to answer certain charges. In view of the date of Edward IV's confirmation to Epworth it is of course possible that some renewal of this dispute and not sedition led to Malory's imprisonment in 1468. Professor Kittredge cites from a Wells register (Hist. MSS. Comm. 10th Report, App. iii, 183) the pardon of August 24, 1468, from which Malory is excluded. He is also excluded from a later pardon of December 1, 1468, preserved in the same register (H. M. C. Wells MSS. i, 407). Much new biographical information has now (1933) been made available by E. Hicks, *Sir Thomas Malory, His Turbulent Career* (1928) and A. C. Baugh, *Documenting Sir Thomas Malory* in *Speculum* viii (1933) 2. It reveals a curious spiritual cleavage between the Malory of the romance and the Malory of life.

# SOME ASPECTS of MEDIÆVAL LYRIC

THE written lyric of the Middle Ages is generally the work of the minstrel or of the *trouvère*, who represent successive stages in the development of the poet as a self-conscious artist. Both naturally write down their songs; the minstrel to aid his own memory and to preserve a professional stock-in-trade, which he may wish to sell or lend to another; the *trouvère* out of creative vanity, to secure from his friends and from those who come after him the

monumentum ære perennius.

But beyond *trouvère*-song and beyond minstrelsy lies the folk-song out of which they both grew, and which long continues to exist side by side with them. Folk-song is rarely written down, at least until it has already been contaminated with literary elements; and the reconstruction of its primitive features by the disentangling of these elements, with what aid history, psychology, and the comparative study of barbarous peoples may afford, is an important function of the anthropologist. His investigations trace the beginnings of lyric to the instinct of emotional self-expression, rhythmic with those quickened dilations and contractions of the heart which are the physiological accompaniments of emotion. Such expression proves to be

46

readily punctuated by the external rhythms of folk-activities which occupy the limbs and leave the spirit free to brood or to exult; rhythms of labour, in the pull of the oar, the swing of the sickle or the flail, the rock of the cradle, the rise and fall of the batlet, the twisting of the spindle, the throw of the shuttle in the loom; or rhythms of play, when the nervous energies, released from the ordinary claims, are diverted into unremunerative channels, and under the rare stimulus of meat and wine the idle feet of the chorus, grouped around the altar of sacrifice or the fruit-laden tree, break into the uplifting of the dance.

The primitive method of folk-song may have been that of mere improvisation, bringing something of definite form and content into half-inarticulate outcry and gradually yielding place in its turn to habits of more deliberate composition. At a very early stage the differentiation must have established itself between the leader of retentive memory and nimble resource, who sets the strain, and the throng who listen and beat time, until the recurring moments when they get the signal to strike in with some rehearsed or familiar burden. And as functions are distinguished and the original homogeneity of the folk begins to break up, it is from the song-leader that the minstrel, and after the minstrel the *trouvère*, takes his starting-point and establishes himself as the recognised exponent of the old songs and the recognised 'maker' of the new. Obviously during this process the depend-

47

ence of poetry upon the throng gradually disappears. The rhythms of the *trouvère's* verses are marked, not by the pulse of flying feet, but by the chords of viol or of lute; and the emotions which dictate them tend more and more to become personal instead of communal, those which a man tells to his own heart in solitude, rather than those which he is moved to cry aloud in company by his sympathy with the crowd of which he forms a part. The burden or *refrain*, no longer an essential element of the song, drops out of use or is retained solely as a literary ornament. But in its survival it is significant of its origin. The forms of art are conservative; and, with whatever change of temper and intention, the *trouvère*, and even more the minstrel, who is far less completely disengaged from the folk than the *trouvère*, is apt to continue the themes and conventions which were first shaped by the folk and still, through all modifications, carry their birth-marks upon them. One other feature of the transition is notable. Art-poetry, whether of the minstrel or the *trouvère* variety, is mainly, if not wholly, masculine poetry. The relation of the minstrel to the *comitatus*, the literary advantage of the clerk, are perhaps sufficient between them to account for this. But it involves a distinct breach with the traditions of the folk, for whom woman, not man, is the characteristic singer. This also is intelligible, since woman's are the greater number of the more leisured and rhythmical of the folk-occupations, and to her, the primitive sower of the seed and planter of herbs, has always been assigned a recognised part in that persistent ritual of agriculture, at whose high seasons the festival excitement finds its ready outlet in the dance.

The earliest written love-poetry of the northern *trouveres* discovers art-song in the very act of passing out of the *cantica diabolica amatoria et turpia* of *rustici* and *rusticanæ* in the *ballationes* of their holiday *chori*, which for centuries past had been a scandal to the discipline of the Church and which a preacher, who may be Cæsarius of Arles, does not hesitate to denounce as a survival of the *observatio paganorum*.[1] The moment is so fundamental for the understanding of all subsequent literature in England as well as in France, that it is important to dwell upon it. The second half of the twelfth century, in which the texts begin, already acknowledges the establishment under Provençal influence of that official *chanson d'amour* or *chanson courtois*, which ultimately succeeded in impressing itself upon the imagination of the Renaissance no less than upon that of the Middle Ages, and may be said to have fixed the type of literary romantic sentiment from the *Canzoniere* of Petrarch to *The Angel in the House*. The characteristics of this poetry are familiar enough. It has practically but one theme, that of the *amour courtois* or *fine amour*; which it expounds with a literary skill and frequent

[1] See the series of prohibitions quoted in my *Mediæval Stage*, 1, 161.

49

delicacy of feeling, that do not save it in the end from the reproach of being cloistered, or from the monotony inseparable from the repeated treatment of the same situation in the light of the same ideals.

> Qu'onques ne fis chançon jor de ma vie,
> Se fine amor nel m'enseigna avant.
>
> (Gace Brulé, xiii, 3.)

The love of the *trouvère* is conceived on the analogy of feudal relations. He vows himself to the service of a mistress, who becomes his liege lady. He is in her *baillie*, her *seignorie*. He must render her the submission of a vassal, and his devotion is amply rewarded by any favour she may choose to bestow upon him. Moreover his loyalty implies not only submission but endurance. His love is for life, and there must be no turning aside. He must love *sens trichier*, through absence, through cruelty, through the misrepresentations of the *gent malparlière*, a terrible folk—

> Qu'a maint amant ont fait ire et oltrage.
>
> (Renals de Couci, ed. Brakelmann, vii, 38.)

The lady, indeed, is most often unkind, and love has to be its own reward. Then the poets go pensively, for love has them in prison, and their songs are sad with tears. But they love on, all the same.

> J'aim par costume et par us,
> La, ou je ne puis ataindre.
>
> (Blondels de Nesle, ed. Brakelmann, xi, 1.)

They are but as children crying for stars; and they know it.

> Empris ai greignor folie
> Que li fols enfes qui crie
> Por la bele estoile avoir,
> Qu'il voit halt el ciel seoir.
>
> (Renals de Couci, iv, 5.)

But they are glad to have it so; they glory in their foolishness, for after all foolishness is only another name for loyalty.

> Coment que je m'en desespoir,
> Bien m'a amors guerredoné,
> Ce que je l'ai a mon pooir
> Servie senz deslealté,
> Que roi m'a fait de folie.
>
> (Renals de Couci, iv, 9.)

Tradition has it that the object of the *trouvère's* worship was often the wife of the patron who protected his art. Certainly there is much deference in the *chansons* to the great romantic exemplar of Tristan and Iseult at the court of King Mark. But since the *trouvère* was not prone to conceal his verses, and since, without any assumption of a particularly high moral standard at courts under the ægis of Eleanor of Aquitaine, it is obvious that patronage has its limits, the conclusion suggests itself that in many cases *amour courtois* must have been a literary convention rather than a passionate reality. This indeed is a problem which recurs at many later stages in the history of amorous poetry; and it stands to reason that no solution of universal application can ever be found for it. The actual formulas of the *chansons*, like those of the Elizabethan sonnets, may cover a variety of personal relations, from somewhat shameless intrigue to married chastity. There were Donnes and Habingtons already in the twelfth century. Equally well there may be nothing to cover but a mere courtly game. In any case this literature is generally reticent, so far as regards the expression of the physical side of love. It is an exception when a *trouvère* writes on the eve of a crusade—

> Or me laist Deus en tel honor monter,
> Que cele ou j'ai mon cuer et mon penser
> Tiegne une nuit entre mes braz nuete,
> Ains que j'aille oltre mer!

(Renals de Couci, VIII, 5.)

There is not even much insistence upon corporeal beauty. Many stanzas are devoted to refining on the psychology of love, and but comparatively few to the celebration of the *bels gens cors* and the *bel oir vair et riant et cler*. The whole literature, indeed, for all its undeniable grace and charm, is self-conscious. The *trouvères* are more in love with love than with their mistresses. They will die, of course, unless the lady shows *merci*; but they take a long time doing it, and in the meantime they find consolation in thinking out intricate arrangements of rhyme for their verses, and sending them abroad to make known their sufferings and their constancy to others of the select few who, like themselves, are sworn to the cult of the *bels sires Deus*.

Euphuism ever walks hand in hand with Romance, and there is significance in the phrases which Blondels de Nesle finds to sum up the ideal of himself and his fellows.

> A la joie apartient
> D'amer molt finement,
> Et, quant li lius en vient,
> Li doners largement;
> Encor plus i covient
> Parler cortoisement;
> Qui ces trois voies tient
> Ja n'ira malement.
>
> (Blondels de Nesle, xiv, 9.)

How far all this is from the folk! not only because folk-song is never self-conscious and never desires to convert the natural way of a man with a maid into mere sentiment, but also because the whole relation between the sexes, as it is represented in the *chansons*, could only have been imagined in the artificial social conditions of courts, wherein it is possible for the real economic subjection of women to be glossed over with an appearance of consideration and respect. The *amour courtois*, in which man is a suppliant, is not the love of the folk, in which the cry for love and the service of love are always on the side of the woman, any more than it is the purged love of the future between two independent human souls coming together out of the depths of their dignity and their isolation.

But the *chanson courtois* does not exhaust the possibilities of mediæval French love-poetry.

Existing side by side with it in the twelfth century, even outliving it and enduring into and beyond the Renaissance, we find another strain of song, which may be distinguished as the *chanson populaire*. This, according to M. Gaston Paris, probably came into existence in the region of Poitou and Limousin, and represents a stock out of which the more developed art-poetry of Provence itself, no less than that of Northern France, had its origin. Little of it can be assigned to famous or even to known *trouvères*; much of it is anonymous and may be in part the work of minstrels. Its themes and forms differentiate themselves very clearly from those of the *chanson courtois*. A notable feature is afforded by the dance-songs, called in the earlier documents *rotrouenges* and in the later *chansons de carole*, *rondets*, or *rondets de carole*. Of these there must once have been many, but only a few dating from the twelfth or early thirteenth century are preserved in their entirety; the rest solely through their *refrains* or burdens, which are freely adapted and quoted in *chansons* of other types and in romances. The burden is of course essential to the dance-song. The primitive form may have consisted of nothing but single lines of text alternating with the burden. Afterwards the number of lines in the *couplet* or stanza was increased, and one or more of these was made to rhyme with the burden. So long as it continued to be popular, the *rondet* retained great freedom of arrangement; ultimately, through its adoption for musical purposes, it became in its turn literary and hardened into fixed forms, such as the *rondel* and the *balade*. The documents seem to distinguish from the *chansons de carole* a group of poems known as *chansons d'histoire*, which tell short love-stories in assonant stanzas with burdens, and bear a close analogy to the English and Scottish ballads. It is not quite clear in what exactly the distinction consists. Possibly the *chansons d'histoire* are in origin just dance-songs with a narrative instead of a purely lyrical content. But they are also sometimes called *chansons de toile*, and in the twelfth century they appear to have been ordinarily sung, not at a dance, but by a company of women over their needlework. In any case it must not be assumed that the *chansons de carole* were never narrative. The extant *refrains* are mostly lyrical, but there are also fragments dealing with the adventures of certain popular personages; with Robin, the typical rustic lover, with 'la bien faite Aalis', with Emmelot, whose mother kept her at home from the dance—

> C'est la jus c'on dit es pres,
> Jeu et bal i sont criés;
> Enmelos i veut aler,
> A sa mere en aquiert gres.
> Par dieu, fille, vous n'ires,
> Trop y a de bachelers.

> (Bartsch, ii, 90.)

From dance-songs may perhaps have been developed the *aubes*, lyric dialogues of lovers parting in the morning, into which is often introduced the cry of the *gaite* or watchman from the castle hard by. But the greater number of the *chansons populaires* belong to a class which may perhaps be best described as *chansons d'aventure*. These are not, as they stand, dance-songs, and although they often use burdens, these are not essential to their structure. They have a narrative setting. The poet tells how he went abroad, generally on a spring morning, and what befell him by the way. Sometimes his part is limited to that of a reporter. In one group of poems, known as the *chansons de mal mariée* he overhears a woman's complaint against married life. In others it is the love-song of a girl, or her regret at having no lover, or at the absence of her lover, or at her immurement in a nunnery. But sometimes he is himself more directly concerned in the adventure. He takes part in a dialogue; or in a very common and widespread type of such poetry he makes love, and after good or ill success rides away.

The distinction between the *chanson courtois* and the *chanson populaire* must not be pressed into an absolute one. We have not here to do with folk-song in the strict sense. The tokens of the castle are clear enough. The *aube* has its *gaite* in the background. The maidens of the *chansons d'histoire* work silken embroideries in a bower. The singers of the *chansons d'aventure* describe themselves as *chevaliers* or *vassals*. Even the dance-songs probably come to us from those *caroles* which the same documents

that preserve their burdens record as an amusement of high society.

> Es ombres sont aléez dessous les oliviers.
> La karole commenchent que les cors ont legiers
> > (*Gui de Nanteuil*, 2441.)

says one romancer; and another—

> Dames et chevaliers ensemble se meslerent
> Et pristrent main à main, et puis si carolerent,
> Et grassieusement deus des dames chanterent.
> > (*Brun de la Montaigne*, 1838.)

What one claims for the *chanson populaire* is, not
that it is folk-song, but that it rests upon folk-song,
and that the forms and motives which it adapts still
inevitably reflect the manners and the sentiments
of the folk by whom they were fashioned. What,
indeed, are the *caroles* of lords and ladies themselves
but the survival under altered social conditions of
precisely those *ballationes vel saltationes aut caraulae*
of village girls against which the Church had for
so many centuries made war? They have features
common in folk-dances to this day. They are
danced hand to hand, in a *ronde* or ring. They have
leaders and a chorus, who divide the song and the
burden between them. They are in the open air, on
a lawn 'dessous les oliviers'. Students of social
history have noticed that in the earlier documents
women alone take part in the *caroles*. That is
significant, when the place of women in folk-
literature is borne in mind. And it is precisely in
keeping with the general character of the *chanson
populaire*, which invariably and in complete con-

tradiction to the tone of the *chanson courtois* approaches love from the woman's point of view. The yearning, the surrender, the rapture, the endurance, the submission, the regret of woman's love; these are the arguments throughout of *chansons d'histoire*, of *aubes*, and of *refrains*. I have not of course forgotten that the great bulk of the literature before us is made up of *chansons d'aventure*, and that in these, at least, the man speaks. It is precisely at this point that the process of adapting folk-themes to the needs of a masculine art-poetry betrays itself. And surely the disguise is transparent enough, if you bear in mind that in the simplest and probably the earliest type of *chanson d'aventure*, that to which M. Jeanroy gives the name of *chanson dramatique*, the minstrel or *trouvère*, as already pointed out, is nothing more than a mere reporter. All that he contributes is the briefest of narrative introductions, and the substance of the song remains the passion or complaint of a woman which he has overheard—

> L'autrier aloie pensant
> A un chant
> Que je fis.
> Trouvai dame soupirant
> Et criant
> A haus cris.
> Tout ainsi, ce m'est avis,
> S'escria—
> > Li jalous
> > Envious
> > De corrous
> > Morra;

Et li dous
Savourous
Amourous
M'avra.

(Bartsch, 1, 51.)

One can hardly doubt that the judgement of M. Gaston Paris is sound, when he puts together this dominant note of womanhood in the *chanson populaire* and the spring settings which the *chansons d'aventure* affect, and finds the well-head of French amorous poetry in the spring festivals, largely celebrated by women, which remain deeply rooted in European agricultural custom as it survives in countless observances of Midsummer or May.[1] Remembering the ecclesiastical pronouncements, he goes on to suggest that to the tradition of such days belonged something of sexual licence inherited from earlier stages of ethical development, and that the 'regina avrilloza' of the Limousin *carole* claimed, as it were, by right to bid defiance to the 'jelos', and to solace herself with the 'leugier bachelar'. Perhaps too much stress should not be laid upon this. Folk-song may become wanton, especially upon a holiday, without being consciously or unconsciously atavistic. The fact remains, however, that the reticence of the *chanson courtois* finds no echo in the sensuous and unabashed temper of the *chanson populaire*—

Soufres, maris, et si ne vous anuit,
Demain m'ares et mes amis anuit.

[1] Cf. *Mediæval Stage*, Book II.

59

Je vous deffenc k'un seul mot n'en parles;
Soufres, maris, et si ne vous mouves,
La nuis est courte, a par mains me rares,
     Qant mes amis ara fait sen deduit.

     Soufres, maris, et si ne vous anuit,
Demain m'ares et mes amis anuit.

(Bartsch, 1, 22.)

It is full-blooded southern love, abandoning itself
beneath the white moon and to the music of the
nightingale, such as startles one on the very
threshold of European literature in the *Pervigilium
Veneris*, and burns still, after how many centuries,
in the heart-throbs of the great Provençal *alba*—

Bels dous amics, fassam un joc novel,
Ins el jardi on chanton li auzel,
Tro la gaita toque son caramel.
     Oi Deus, oi Deus, de l'alba! Tan tost ve!

(Bartsch, *Chrest. Prov.* 1, 109.)

The nightingale, indeed, plays a conspicuous part in
all this poetry. His song is the symbol of amorous
passion, and he himself is appealed to as the
confident and adviser of lovers, the go-between who
bears messages from heart to heart. He has a right
to his place, for in France his coming, like that of
the swallow in Greece, the stork in Germany, and
the cuckoo in England, is the signal to the folk that
summer is at hand, and that the time for the high
revel has come.

Naturally enough, the courtly adapters have
drawn more freely upon the amorous elements in

the festival songs than upon the invocations of the
summer itself which accompanied them in the
village ritual. But examples of these also are to be
found in the rich store of *refrains* preserved in the
singular romance of *Guillaume de Dole*. One of
these is specifically described as sung on May
morning by citizens who 'aporterent lor mai' from
the wood—

> Tout la gieus sor rive mer,
> Compaignon, or dou chanter.
> Dames i ont bauz levez:
> Mout en ai le cuer gai.
> Compaignon, or dou chanter
> En l'onor de mai.

(v, 4154.)

The other is of precisely similar character—

> Tendez tuit voz mains a la flor d'esté,
> A la flor de liz.
> Por Deu, tendez i.

(v, 5099.)

These complete the connection of the *caroles* and
the *chanson populaire* to which they belong with the
folk-festivals. To them, one may conjecture, originally belonged the title of *reverdie*, song of
earth's *renouveau*, which in fact is used in a more
general sense as indicating a light-hearted ditty.
It is to be observed that the descriptive passages,
of blossoming trees and luting birds, which occur
in the introductions to the *chansons d'aventure*, are
just of the nature to be expected on the theory
that these represent an adaptation of the manner

of more primitive spring songs. The original *chanson* has no need to explain its own circumstances. But the adapter strives to reproduce the environment as well as the theme, and it is only in his narrative setting that he can do this. The same principle may be pushed further. A large number of those *chansons d'aventure* which are not purely *chansons dramatiques* have a character which has earned them the name of *pastourelles*. The scenes are placed amongst shepherds and shepherdesses; and is not this precisely because it was amongst shepherds and shepherdesses that the literary models of which the poets are making use were found? You have to deal with a deliberate attempt to preserve local colour. The *pastourelle*, one feels, is the most sophisticated variety of the *chanson populaire*, the nearest to the *chanson courtois*. The authors are already a long way from the folk when they begin to make pictures of it like this. In the substance of the poems, too, the class-distinction between the *vassal* and the *pastorel* is very clearly felt. And the courtly temper of minstrel and *trouvère* is beginning to remould the folk-material. The poet now sings more often of his own love than of a woman's love overheard. And it is a light love; the seriousness of the folk-poetry, with its strain of elemental passion, is relaxed. Quite a number of *pastourelles* are by known *trouvères* who have taken part in the *chanson courtois* itself. They have their *aventures* as they come and go *pensis com fins amourous*. Apparently a passage with

Marion or Ermenjon was no bar to *aimer sens trichier*, although it is to the credit of Jehans Erars that he refused an *amor novele* even when offered in such circumstances. Technically, again, the *pastourelle* is freely handled. It uses a burden or not, at pleasure. Often a number of *refrains* occur in a single piece; an arrangement which implies a clear departure from the original choric intention which produced the *refrain*. Or for sung words is substituted a *dorenlot*, or nonsense-burden, a collection of inarticulate syllables, such as 'turuluruta' or 'chivalala', meant as a conventional imitation of the notes of a rustic pipe. Here, once more, is the device of an adapter.

If, now, we accept the *chanson populaire* as a half-way stage in the movement of the poetic impulse from folk-song to the fully developed art-song represented by the *chanson courtois*, it becomes apparent that even the *chanson courtois* itself is not wholly forgetful of its remoter past. Atmosphere and sentiment have changed until they are hardly recognisable; but the tradition of the spring setting still endures, and as of old it is the nightingale who, in the *renouveau* of all things, calls upon the poet also to renew, no longer the glad hymn of anticipated foison, but the sad plaining of a cherished love which may neither attain nor die.

> Li roisignors anonce la novele
> Que la saisons del dolz tens est venue,
> Que tote riens renaist et renovele,
> Que li pré sont covert d'erbe menue.

63

Por la saison, qui se change et remue,
Chascuns, fors moi, s'esjoïst et revele;
Las! car si m'est changie la merele,
Qu'on m'a geté en prison et en mue!

(Blondels de Nesle, xiii, 1.)

Art, indeed, is at once the most revolutionary and the most conservative of human activities.

The perversity of history renders it impossible to trace any direct development of art-song out of folk-song in England analogous to that which took place in France. There is no post-classical European poetry older than that of the Anglo-Saxons; but this, in its surviving texts, is already clear of the folk. A small and early portion of it is the work of minstrels interested in epic and the glorification of kings; the bulk has taken on a uniformly religious and didactic colouring at the hands of clerks. There is no love-poetry, and the nearest approach to lyric is in certain reflective pieces more properly to be called elegiac. They are philosophic poems, broodings over life in its entirety, rather than expressions of its passionate moments of joy and sorrow, and they have a well-defined tendency towards pessimism which impresses itself as a distinctive note of the Anglo-Saxon temper. Life really is a serious thing to these dwellers in a desolate region. It gives little joy when it is here, save the stern joy of battle, and it rapidly passes into nothingness. One recalls Bede's image of the sparrow flying into the radiant hall and out again into the whirl of frost and snow from whence it came. There is little hint of folk-song beyond a few historic lays, and at the Conquest the vernacular goes underground for a couple of centuries, and England becomes for literary purposes a province of France. From the blossoming time of the *chanson populaire* and the *chanson courtois* no English secular lyric is preserved to us, although Giraldus Cambrensis affords testimony in an amusing story to its existence.

Exemplum de sacerdote, qui in Anglia Wigorniae finibus his nostris diebus interiectam quandam cantilenae particulam, ad quam saepius redire consueverant, quam refectoriam seu refractoriam [*refrain*] vocant, ex reliquiis cogitationum, et quoniam ex abundantia cordis os loqui solet, quia tota id nocte in choreis circiter ecclesiam ductis audierat, mane ad missam sacerdotalibus indutus, et ad aram stans insignitus, pro salutatione ad populum, scilicet *Dominus vobiscum*, eandem Anglica lingua coram omnibus alta voce modulando pronuntiavit in hunc modum, *Swete lamman dhin are.* Cuius haec dicti mens esse potest, *Dulcis amica, tuam poscit amator opem.* Huius autem eventus occasione episcopus loci illius, Willelmus scilicet de Norhale [1184–90], sub anathematis interminatione publice per synodos et capitula prohiberi fecit, ne cantilena illa, propter memoriae refricationem, quae ad mentem facinus revocare potest, de caetero per episcopatum suum caneretur.

The latter part of the thirteenth century brings three snatches, caught up, as was so often the case in France itself at this time, into musical settings. Two of these are laments, probably amorous in character and still impregnated with the Anglo-Saxon melancholy; the third, the famous *Cuckoo Song*, is not folk-song, but a learned composer's adaptation of a *reverdie* or chant of welcome to the spring. Finally, just at the beginning of the fourteenth century, comes a sudden group of poems of and about love, most of which form part of a miscellaneous collection gathered out of French, Latin, and various dialects of English, and written down somewhere in the south-west of the country, possibly at Leominster Abbey. With these the silence is broken indeed. The love-songs are those of a man, not a woman. The general tone is closely akin to that of the French *trouvères*. The lovers are parted from their ladies, or these are unkind, and they sing of the pains and yearning of love, rather than of love's exultation. 'Derne love' has them in his 'baundoun'. They 'sorewe ant syke' and 'waxe grene' for love, and will die or 'walke wod' unless they have some comfort. They are thrashed about in the mill-dam of love—

> For wowyng al forwake,
> Wery so water in wore.

The derivation of all this is unmistakable. The nightingale, the *renouveau* of leaf and grass, the sudden remembered pang; all are there—

> When the nyhtègalè singes,
>   The wodès waxen grene,
> Lef ant gras ant blosmè springes
>   In Averyl, I wene;
> Ant love is to myn hertè gon
>   With onè spere so kene,
> Nyht ant day my blod hit drynkes,
>   Myn hertè deth to tene.

66

The song has been sung from Aragon to Arras ere now.

Yet, as compared with the typical *trouvères*, these writers wear their rue with a difference. The ambiguous Platonic relationships of the regular *amour courtois* are missing. The poet is wooing, not a wedded wife, but a 'byrd' or a 'mai', and his will is clearly for the natural end of unsophisticated love. He is frank enough about it—

> Hevene y tolde al his
> That o nyht were hire gest.

There are little personal touches. One 'wommon woneth by west'; the country-side wherein another hath no equal is 'bituené Lyncolne ant Lyndeseye, Norhamptoun ant Lounde'. The hawthorn name of this is Alysoun, of that Johon. And there is a good deal more of physical description than the courtly *trouvères*, always intent upon the metaphysics of love to the disregard of its sensuous aspects, allow themselves. It is the serene western type—

> With lossom eyé, grete and gode,
> With browen blysfol under hode.

The 'bel oil vair' of *chanson* and romance is repeated in 'that sweté thing, with eyenen gray'; but Alysoun has black eyes which contrast with her fair hair and brown brows. A damsel of Ribbesdale is depicted with the precision of a miniature—

> Hire hed when ich biholde upon,
> The sonnébeem abouté noon
> Me thohté that y seye;

Hyre eyyen aren grete ant gray ynoh,
Ant lussum, when heo on me loh,
   Ybend wax eyther breye.

   .    .    .    .

Heo hath browės bend an heh,
Whyt bytuene ant nout to neh,

   .    .    .    .

Hire chyn ys cloven, ant eyther cheke
Whit ynoh ant rode on eke,
   Ase rosė when hit redes.

Heo hath a mury mouht to mele,
With lefly redė lippės lele,
   Romaunz forte rede.

   .    .    .    .

Hyre tyttės aren an under bis
As apples tuo of parays,
   Ou self ye mowen seo.

This becomes a detestable way of writing later on, with the seventeenth-century cataloguers of feminine charms, but in the fourteenth century it at any rate shows that the poet has his eye on the object.

The lines just quoted form part of a *chanson d'aventure*, and another poem in the manuscript belongs definitely to the same type. It is a dialogue in which the singer finds 'a wel fayer fenge' in a 'fryht', woos her, and is bidden to 'go his gates' exactly as in a *pastourelle*. Certainly the English poems have their affinities to the *chanson populaire* as well as to the *chanson courtois*. They derive, indeed, not from the courtly heyday of *trouvère* poetry so much as from the aftermath, itself touched with popular elements, which was produced amongst the great *bourgeois* towns of Northern France. It was with the Adans de la Hale, not the Thibauts de Champagne, that our monk was in touch during the *wanderjahre* in which he first heard the songs that he afterwards wrote down amongst the apple-blossoms of his Herefordshire priory. And his gatherings contain more than one of those controversial pieces for and against womanhood, which were the outcome of a sceptical *bourgeois* reaction against the rigorous idealism of the *amour courtois*. The authors of his poems probably belonged, like himself and like Adan de la Hale, to the order of *clerici vagantes*. It is a clerk and not a *chevalier* for whom the lady of a dialogue is ready to defy 'fader, moder, and al my kun'. And thus may be explained the trilingual character of the collection, culminating in lines which are illuminating almost to the point of autobiography.

> *Dum ludis floribus velut lacinia,*
> Le dieu d'amour me tient en tiel *angustia*;
> Merour me tient de duel e de *miseria,*
> Si je ne la ay *quam amo super omnia.*
>
> *Ejus amor tantum me facit fervere,*
> Qe je ne soi *quid possum inde facere*;
> Pur ly covent *hoc saeculum relinquere,*
> Si je ne pus l'amour de li *perquirere.*
>
> Ele est si bele e gente dame *egregia,*
> Cum ele fust *imperatoris filia*;
> De beal semblant *et pulcra continencia*
> Ele est la flur *in omni regis curia.*

69

Quant je le vey, je su *in tali gloria,*
Come est la lune *coeli inter sidera.*
Dieu la moi doint *sua misericordia*
Beyser et fere *quae secuntur alia*!

*Scripsi haec carmina in tabulis;*
Mon ostel est en mi la vile de Paris.
May y sugge namore, so wel me is!
Yef hi deye for love of her, duel hit ys.

(Wright, *S.L.P.* xxiii.)

To the ecclesiastical training of the writers may
perhaps be ascribed certain touches of pedantic
symbolism, whereby a mistress is designated in a
string of tropes as 'lilie of largesse, parvenke of
prouesse, selsecle of suetnesse', and the like, after
a manner familiar in hymns to the Virgin.

It remains to be asked how far the fourteenth-
century poems give a distinctively English note,
and whether they can be supposed to draw any
direct inspiration from English folk-song. English
enough is a tendency to alliteration, showing itself
especially in the passages of pedantry just referred
to; and English, I think, is a certain seriousness
and brooding melancholy which affords love-
ecstasies more convincing either than the conventions of the *trouvères* or than the *chansons d'aventure,*
about which there is always a suspicion of Gallic
irony. But these belong to the Anglo-Saxon literary
tradition, and of folk-song there is but little to be
found. There are only two burdens used. One of
these, indeed, may be taken up from folk-song; it
is alien from the poem to which it is attached, and

its motive of woman's love in absence recurs in the
*Western Wind* of a Tudor song-book, and in the
ballad of *The Unquiet Grave*.

> Blow, northerne wynd,
> Sent thou me my suetyng!
> Blow, northerne wynd,
>     Blou, blou, blou!

In another poem the amorous element is sub-
ordinated to a *reverdie* more elaborate, like the
*Cuckoo Song* itself, than is usual in the French
models. But on the whole the poets, with their
masculine love and their rhythmical accomplishment, do not stand very near to the folk. They have
the freshness of the primal world upon them, no
doubt, but after all it is the business of the art-poet
to keep this freshness and yet to sing his own song.
And the sentiment is individual, not communal.
Out of his personal fancy a man writes—

> Ich wolde ich were a threstelcok,
> A bountyng other a laverok,
>     Swetė bryd!
> Bi tuene hire curtel ant hire smok
>     Y wolde ben hyd.

There is a literary past behind one who endeavours
to sum up a thousand poetic introductions in the
single line—

> Lenten ys come with love to toune.

And what curious sympathy with far-off Catullus

shaped this exquisite love-letter across the English cowslips?

> Fayrest fode upo loft,
>> My gode luef, y the greete
> As felė sythe ant oft
>> As dewes dropės beth weete,
>> Ase sterrės beth in welkne ant grasės sour ant suete.

The delightful promise of the Leominster manuscript is, alas! not maintained. The macaronic verses of a Cambridge manuscript are perhaps less interesting for any sheer poetic quality than as a renewed reminder of the cosmopolitan character of mediæval literature. There must have been popular songs in the fourteenth century for Absolon to sing to his rubible, but edacious time has reduced them to tantalising fragments. Amongst aimless scribbles on a blank leaf of Rawlinson MS. D. 913 is the following—

> Icham of Irlaunde and of the holy londe of Irlande.
>> Gode sire, pray ich ye,
>> For of saynte Charite,
> Come ant daunce wyt me in Irlaunde.

We would dance gladly did we but know the tune. Another scrap on the same page has also its air of romantic suggestion—

> Maiden in the mor lay, in the mor lay, sevenyht full.
>> Welle was hire mete, wat was hire mete?
>> The primerole ant the violet.

Of an entire poem in Bodley MS. 692, only the first two lines are legible—

>> Joly cheperte of Aschell down
>> Can more on love than al this town.

72

With the fifteenth century emerge the ballads; but these, although they contain lyric as well as narrative elements, and certainly bring us, in some kind or degree, into contact with the folk, open up too many serious questions for treatment as a side-issue here. An isolated masterpiece, at the end of the century, is *The Nutbrown Maid*. This has affinities to the ballads, to which outlaws and the greenwood are dear; but it is primarily lyric, and may have been written for recitation in alternative chant by two minstrels. Its double burden and the fact that the woman bears the brunt of the emotion hint at an inspiration from folk-song. It continues the tradition also of the Leominster manuscript. There is an advance in freedom of handling and mastery of rhythm; but the ring of sincerity and wholesome conviction is the same. The professed purpose of the poem connects itself with the old dispute as to the qualities of women which the *amour courtois* had provoked. The actual form has its precedent in an earlier dialogue between a lady and a clerk and even the greenwood note is there anticipated.

Literary poetry during the fifteenth century is, of course, wholly under the domination of Chaucer; and Chaucer, English though he is and thoroughly in touch with the folk in *The Canterbury Tales*, does not draw his lyric from native sources. His *balades* and *rondels* represent a fresh wave of continental influence. 'The note, I trowe, ymakèd was in Fraunce.' These are exotic forms, worked out by

French musicians on the basis of the French *caroles*, which became the literary fashion as the *grands chansons* died away. What Chaucer really did was to divert the fifteenth century from lyric to narrative; but so far as Lydgate and Occleve and their fellows write lyric at all, they follow his models and show but little spontaneity. The English versions of poems by Charles of Orleans and others are something of an accident and hardly come into account; and the resource, pungency, and versatility of Skelton were too rarely turned in a lyrical direction. Skelton, however, was contemporary with a renascence of song under the early Tudors, for which we have to thank the musicians. *The Cuckoo Song* and other isolated examples survive to show that the thirteenth-century part-song had its English as well as its continental vogue, and that both courtly and popular poetry were drawn upon to provide secular themes for such compositions. But the great age of English counterpoint was in the fifteenth century, and was due to the growth in importance under the patronage of Henry VI, himself no mean musician, of the domestic choir which maintained the services of the royal chapel. A school of composers arose, of whom the most famous was John Dunstable; and for a while England led the musical development of France and Flanders. The work of this school was mainly religious and largely liturgical, and such of its amorous productions as have survived are unfortunately mutilated. But we owe to it the well-

74

known *Agincourt* song and that of *God Speed the
Plow.*

The merthe of alle this londe
Maketh the gode husbonde,
    With eringe of his plowe.
Iblessed be Cristès sonde,
That hath us sent in honde
    Merthe and joye enowe.

The plowe gothe mony a gate,
Bothe erly and eke late,
    In winter in the clay,
Aboute barly and whete,
That makethe men to swete.
    God spede the plowe all day!

Browne Morel and Gore
Drawen the plowe full sore
    All in the morweninge;
Rewarde hem therefore
With a shefe or more
    Alle in the eveninge.

Whan men biginne to sowe,
Full well here corne they knowe
    In the mounthe of May.
However Janiver blowe
Wether hie or lowe,
    God spede the plowe alle way!

Whan men biginnethe to wede
The thistle fro the sede
    In somer whan they may,
God lete hem well to spede;
And longe gode life to lede,
    Alle that for plowe men pray.

75

After the death of Dunstable the school lost its European hegemony, and became, from a musical point of view, unprogressive. But the habit of composition endured, and song-books of the reigns of Henry VII and Henry VIII show a considerable activity in the setting of light and amorous ditties. Henry VIII had himself some taste for music, although modern critics deny him musical talent; and, with his, the outstanding names are those of Robert Fairfax and William Cornish, both of whom were Gentlemen of the Chapel. It must not, of course, be taken for granted that the authors of settings were necessarily also the authors of the words set. But probably it was so in some cases. Cornish, for example, was certainly a literary man as well as a musician. He was Master of the Children of the Chapel, and in this capacity devised masks and interludes, in which he appeared before the king with his fellows and the children.

It must be admitted that the general character of the Tudor songs is a little disappointing. They hardly foreshadow a new literary age. The Renascence lingers, while they re-echo conventions which have already grown familiar during the mediæval centuries. Here, dressed out in the more complicated harmony of pricksong, are the very vows and laments of *amour courtois*, which the *trouvère* chanted so long ago to the simple accompaniment furnished by the *vielle* of his *jongleur*. Here are bits of the allegory dear to the fourteenth century. Here once again are the overheard complaints of women and the pastoral dialogues of the *chansons d'aventure*. The nightingale is still 'jargonning' in the spring. Courtly and popular elements appear in about equal degree. Burdens are not unusual; the Amyas snatch of Cornish's allegory seems alien to the structure of the poem, and recalls the greenwood motive of *The Nutbrown Maid* and the ballads.

> You and I and Amyas,
> Amyas and you and I,
> To the green wood we must go, alas!
> You and I, my life, and Amyas.

> The knight knocked at the castle gate;
> The lady marvelled who was thereat.

> To call the porter he would not blin;
> The lady said he should not come in.

> The portress was a lady bright;
> Strangèness that lady hight.

> She asked him what was his name;
> He said 'Desire, your man, madame'.

> She said 'Desire, what do ye here?'
> He said 'Madame, as your prisoner'.

> He was counselled to brief a bill,
> And show my lady his own will.

> 'Kindness', said she, 'would it bear',
> 'And Pity', said she, 'would be there'.

> Thus how they did we can not say;
> We left them there and went our way.

Looking back on the Leominster manuscript and comparing its temper with that of the Tudor lyrists, one is conscious of a loss of seriousness and con-

77

viction. 'Derne love' has given place to the light love of a frivolous court, where you wear your heart upon your sleeve and must not have the ill manners to let real feeling spoil the game. Irresponsible lightheartedness—'Pastime with good company', as Henry put it—is the ideal of the day. The deeper accents of emotion, with much else that is of the soul of literature, come back with Wyatt; but Wyatt, though he rubbed elbows with the writers of the song-books, lies outside the scope of these observations.

The English religious lyric of the Middle Ages far exceeds in bulk that of the love-lyric. And it declares itself earlier. Some twelfth-century fragments pass under the name of St Godric, once a sea-roving chapman and afterwards a hermit of Finchale in Durham. The thirteenth and early fourteenth centuries afford quite a respectable harvest in half a dozen manuscripts, including that of Leominster already dwelt upon.[1] One of these comes from as far as Kildare, in Ireland, and is written in an Anglo-Irish dialect. The dominant feature of this poetry is its elegiac quality. It takes its impulse from the contemplation of things as a whole and the conviction of their inherent uncertainty. It is full of the vanity of life and the nothingness of man—

Of this worldes ioie, hou hit geth al to noght.

[1] More now (1933); cf. Carleton Brown, *Religious Lyrics of the Fourteenth Century* (1928), and *English Lyrics of the Thirteenth Century* (1932).

It abounds in metaphors for the fleeting character
of human happiness, which glides away 'also the
schadewe' or 'so wyndes bles' or 'so the scheft is
of the cleo'. The world is 'bot a brotil tre' and 'the
ax is at the rote'. It 'faleweth so doth medowe
gras', as said the Psalmist—

> This world is love is gon awai,
> So dew on grasse in somer is dai.

Glories and splendours may not endure. As to the
rest, so the message is to those—

> that sittet ischrud
> With skarlet and with palle.

The laughter of youth, the beauty of woman, the
strength of knight and baron, the state of queens;
all must vanish. Where are the great sovereigns and
the great lovers of the past?

> Hwer is Paris and Heleyne,
>   That weren so bryht and feyre on bleo?
> Amadas, Tristram and Dideyne,
>   Yseude and allé theo,
> Ector with his scharpé meyne,
>   And Cesar riche of worldés feo?
> Heo beoth iglyden ut of the reyne,
>   So the scheft is of the cleo.

*Ubi nunc fidelis ossa Fabricii manent?* Boethius had
asked the question long ago; and long afterwards
it resounds in Villon's famous *ballade*, and even in
the song of Elizabethan Nashe—

> Queens have died young and fair;
> Dust hath closed Helen's eye.

79

It is all vanity, saith the poet, as the preacher had said before him. Even 'Henry ure kyng', no less than Absalon, shall be dimmed—

> Ne may hit never his waraunt beo,
> Gold ne seolver, vouh ne gray.

Man is no more than earth upon earth, and the phrase becomes the text of a whole group of poems, linking themselves with that favourite pictorial representation of mediæval pessimism, the Dance of Death. The singer dwells with grim interest upon the last tragic horrors of mortality, when the rosy flesh is but 'wermes fode', and man 'that was so modi and so strong' is impotent on his bier any longer to protect his own—

> Nu lith the clei-clot
> Al so the ston,
> And his freondes striveth
> To gripen his iwon.

And after death comes the judgement. The future is dark in the next world, as in this—

> I not whider I shal, ne hou longe her duelle.

There is the 'murie londe', but there is also the dread alternative of—

> the lothe hous
> That to the fende is wrohte.

It is perhaps a consolation that even in these grim

regions the irony of fate pursues the great ones of
the earth, no less than common folk.

> Moni of thissè riche,
>     That wereden foh and grei,
> An rideth uppè stede
> And uppen palefrai,
> Heo schulen attè dome
>     Suggen weilawei.

*Weilawei!* It is the keynote, the constantly iterated
burden, of all this *macabre* desperate song.

Professedly it is Christian poetry, but the colour
of its sentiment is no essential part of the Christian
attitude towards life. Perhaps we have to do with a
matter of racial temperament rather than of creed,
and it is the Anglo-Saxon melancholy that inspires
so keen a sense of the transitoriness and uncertainty
of all mortal things. It speaks, as it were, with the
least qualification in a lullaby of the Kildare manuscript. By this sad lilt the very child in his cradle
is taught that sorrow is the law of life. Weeping he
comes into the world, and with good cause, for the
world will be his foe, as it has ever been the foe of
his 'eldren'. His foot is in the wheel, and he is
beginning a pilgrimage, at the end of which death
out of 'a wel dim horre' awaits him. It is the very
cry of pagan Lear, as he feels the foundations of
his life crumbling around him—

> Thou knowest, the first time that we smell the air,
> We wawl and cry...
> When we are born, we cry that we are come
> To this great stage of fools.

Of course, it is largely a matter of emphasis. Even the lullaby takes its Christian turn; it is through Adam's apple and the wickedness of Satan that death came into the world. And the consciousness of the vanity of things fits in well enough with one aspect of Christian doctrine. It is a reading of life which Christianity had had to meet and to absorb into itself at an earlier stage. The poets, as we have seen, could draw from the *Psalms* and from *Ecclesiastes*. They could draw also from more than one patristic writing *De Contemptu Mundi*. A more immediate source is the so-called *Poema Morale*, which dates from the second half of the twelfth century. This is not cast in lyric form, but the lyrics repeat many of its ideas and its phrases. It is a poem of regret for a misspent life, which expands into an exposition of the last things and of the scheme of salvation. Obviously the sentiment becomes more definitely Christian when the philosophical despair is supplemented by a sense of personal sin, and still more when the hope of redemption is suggested as a consolation. The lullaby lacks both of these, but the latter at least is seldom altogether omitted in a thirteenth-century lyric. Only it is present in different proportions. Sometimes there is a mere perfunctory bidding of Christ or the Virgin to be 'bote', in a final stanza, which hardly affects the tenour of the whole; sometimes this element is elaborated, until the pessimism and even the expression of personal contrition fall into the background, and the poem takes the shape of a hymn or

a prayer. Herewith comes in, directly or through
the French, the influence of Latin hymnology,
which supplies models both for structure and for
diction. At this stage the appeal is generally to
Christ and the Virgin themselves, rather than to the
saints. An address to 'holy Thomas of heoveriche'
as 'help in Engelaunde' is quite exceptional. And
the approach is a direct one; there is little flavour
of ecclesiasticism, or dwelling on church and
sacraments as avenues of grace. Certain objective
elements of description and incident begin to make
their appearance with such themes as the Annuncia-
tion, the *Stabat Mater*, and the Five Joys of Mary.
It can hardly be said that the ethical tone of the
lyrics is strenuous. The monastic shrinking from
the world is more in evidence than the virile desire
to conquer it. The soul is too often content with a
passive acquiescence in its own salvation through
the merits of others; and one welcomes the rarer
intervention of a more vigorous temper—

> Oup, and be god champioun!
> Stond, ne fal namore adoun
> For a luytel blast!

Other examples of individual lyric emotion dis-
engaging itself from the common theme are afforded
by two poems in the Leominster manuscript, which
are imitations, but not translations, of the *Iesu,
dulcis memoria!* of St Bernard of Clairvaux. Here the
feeling of personal adoration breaks away from the
formal 'bidding', and the burden of the whole is
the constant motive of the mystics, the passion of the

soul for the divine object. The aspiration is not merely for salvation at the end, but for the love of Christ for its own sake, as an abiding comfort here and now.

The dependence of the English upon the Latin hymns would be unmistakable, even without the tags of Latin which indicate a habit of translating the couplets of a caudated poem, while leaving the *caudæ* themselves in the original. It is even more interesting to trace a very distinct influence of the contemporary secular lyric. Thus the Virgin is addressed, not only by such obvious names as 'Moder milde', 'Maiden moder', 'Moder and virgyne', or by the symbolic appellations of 'Quene of evene', 'Quene of storre', 'Flur of parays', and the like, but also in language bearing the closest resemblance to that which the *trouvères* were in the habit of addressing to their mistresses. She is 'Mi leové sweté lefdi' or 'Lavedi so fair and so hende'. One poet calls her—

> My dayés blis, my nyhtés rest.

Another sings—

> Nou is fre that er was thral,
> Al thourh that levedy gent ant smal.

Nor do the parallels stop here. The structure and conventions of amorous poetry are deliberately adapted and turned to pious uses in songs of spiritual love-longing, *chansons d'aventure* of the soul.

> Ase y me rod this ender day
> By grené wodé to seche play,
> Mid herte I thohte al on a may,
> Suetest of allé thinge.

84

The 'may' is the Virgin, and the poem goes on to tell of her Five Joys. For these poets the old setting of the *renouveau* has found a new meaning.

> When y se blosmės springe,
>    Ant herė foulės song,
> A suetė lovė longynge
>    Myn hertė thourh out stong;
> Al for a lovė newe,
> That is so suete ant trewe,
>    That gladieth al mi song.

But it is Jesus whom the singer has 'cheosen to lemmon'. In another piece the theme of 'Somer is comen and winter gon' is similarly diverted, while in the Leominster manuscript a love-song and its religious parody are preserved side by side. Such give and take between the divine and the secular is of course no rarity in literature. It were easy to quote examples from the comedies of Hrotsvitha to the *Gude and Godlie Ballatis* and beyond. In the case of the lyrics the earliest intermediaries were doubtless the *scholares vagantes*, who stole mundane melodies for their hymns as readily as they profaned the churches by fitting improper words to the liturgical chants. But by the end of the thirteenth century one has also to take account of the activity of the Franciscan friars, and to remember that St Francis, a *trouvère* in his youth and a poet to the end, was careful to enjoin upon his brothers the duty of becoming *ioculatores Domini* and turning song to the service of heaven. It is at least curious that the only two names to which religious lyrics

85

attach themselves in this century are both those of Minorites. One is that of 'Frere Michel Kyldare' who wrote one at least of the Anglo-Irish poems; the other that of Thomas de Hales, whose *Cantus quem composuit ad instanciam cuiusdam puellae deo dicatae* is perhaps the most complete example of the tendency under discussion. A 'maydė Cristes' has bidden the poet—

> That ich hire wurche a luveron;

and so, after a typical exposition of the vanity of the world, some passages from which I have already had occasion to quote, he advises her to let Christ be her lover—

> Mayde, if thu wilnest after leofmon,
> Ich techė the enne treowė king.

Christ has sent her his 'sonde' and desires 'forto beo the cuth'. All the joys of his 'leovemon', including the 'derewurthe gemme' of 'maydenhod', are set out.

The same strain of religious poetry endured into the fourteenth century. The lyrical element in the Kentish poems of William of Shoreham is of little account. A more significant name is that of the Yorkshire hermit and precursor of Wyclife, Richard Rolle of Hampole, who seems to have adopted the deliberate Minorite practice of endeavouring to sanctify song. 'Nec lira laetitiae quam lubrici laudabant mihi libebat', he says in his barbarous Latin, 'sed et cantum carnalium concito calcavi, ad

Christum convertens quod cantabatur. Cantilenas quidem de feminis facerunt; hoc reputavi rursum ruinam.' Rolle was a systematic mystic, and represents the impulse to sing as an echo of a divine *canor* forming a particular stage in the mystical path. He seems to have begun with short snatches of song interspersed amongst his prose treatises, and afterwards to have expanded these into more elaborate poems, of which a collection is preserved under the name of *Cantica Divini Amoris*. Amongst other pieces assigned to him on conjecture is a lengthened and amalgamated version of the two imitations of St Bernard of Clairvaux in the Leominster manuscript. Whether this conjecture be sound or not, it is precisely the tradition of such poetry that he continues. All his verse is of 'love-longing', filled with that sense of personal contact between the soul and the divine object which appears to lie at the heart of the mystical apprehension. His subjective reading of religion and a certain personal austerity of outlook give him affinities rather to Protestant than to typically Catholic sentiment. He conceives of love, not as softness, but as fire; to him, as to the *trouvères*, although in another sense, it is 'derne love'.

> For now, lufe thow, I redė, Cryste, as I thee tell,
> And with aungels take thy stedė; that joy loke thou noght
>     sell!
> In erth thow hate, I rede, all that thy lufe may fell,
> For luf es stalworth as the dedė, luf es hard as hell.
>
>                 (Horstman, I, 77.)

Rolle's literary quality has perhaps been exaggerated by uncritical admirers. But a vein of real lyric sweetness runs through his rather harsh northern utterance; and even his homeliness of speech is not without its occasional charm.

> Owre setels heven ar within; me lyst sytt in myne,

he says; and the red-litten windows of a Yorkshire farmhouse arise before you as an image of the new Jerusalem. He is often strongly alliterative, and not least in his most objective poem, a meditation on the Passion—

> My fender of my fose sa fonden in the felde,
> Sa lufly lyghtand at the evensang-tyde;
> Thy moder and hir menyhe unlacéd thy scheld;
> All wepéd that thar were, thy woundés was sa wyde.

> (Horstman, I, 72.)

Alliteration is a feature of his Latin also, and he perhaps represents the beginning of a tendency, natural enough as the English folk came more and more into contact with literature, which culminated in the marked alliterative revival by Langland and his fellows at the end of the century. This revival itself touches upon lyric in *Pearl*, although the exquisite threnody is too long and too elegiac to be properly classed as a lyric. Rolle seems to have founded something of a school, through such disciples as William of Nassington; and his influence is the most notable one in the large accumulations of religious poetry garnered in the Thornton, Vernon, Simeon, Lambeth, and other manuscripts of the fifteenth century. Here, however, we may trace a growing ecclesiasticism, together with literary influences which show themselves in elaborate Chaucerian stanza-forms and Latin refrains. The beautiful *Quia Amore Langueo* stands out of a mass of verse of no great moment.

But this amazing fifteenth century, whose official poets sleep so contentedly in the shadow of Chaucer, shows itself, in the less exalted sphere of popular literature, full of surprises. To the miracle plays and the ballads it adds the carols. At the end of a tedious versifying of the whole duty of man by John Awdlay, a blind chaplain of Haghmon, in Shropshire, comes a sudden change of key. The gladdened scribe marks it with red letters—

> I pray yow, sirus, boothe moore and lase,
> Sing these caroles in Cristèmas.

Then follow twenty-five short poems, some at least of which have the genuine lyric ring, while all are shown by their lilting burdens to be intended for utterance in song. One of them is 'mad of King Herrè'; others are on moral themes, or in honour of the Virgin. But there is a group belonging to the range of high feasts which fall in the twelve nights from Nativity to Epiphany; and the introductory couplet makes it sufficiently clear that the primary purpose of the whole collection was for service in the Christmas season. They are, in fact, examples of a kind of song which is familiar in the popular literature of all European countries, and has lasted to quite modern times, in England under Awdlay's very name of carols, and in France under that of *noëls*. Part of Awdlay's volume was composed in the year 1426. Some of the carols may be of rather earlier date. Two of them recur, with many others of similar structure, in an anonymous Sloane manuscript of about the same period. It is convenient and, as will be seen, historically correct, to confine the use of the term carol to short poems, furnished with a burden and intended for singing. Of these the bulk of the Sloane manuscript is made up; but it also contains Latin verses, at least one regular ballad, and a few freely written lyrics, which share the general character of the carols, and are in some cases of rare beauty. That which begins 'I sing of a maiden' is well known, but here is another.

> Adam lay ibounden,
>    Bounden in a bond;
> Four thousand winter
>    Thoght he not too long;
> And all was for an appil,
>    An appil that he tok,
> As clerkės finden
>    Wreten in here book.
> Ne hadde the appil takė ben,
>    The appil taken ben,
> Ne haddė never our lady
>    A ben hevenė quene.
> Blessėd be the time
>    That appil takė was.
> Therefore we moun singen
>    '*Deo gracias*'.

One of the carols preserves historical allusions which suggest that it was written in the last half of the fourteenth, rather than at the beginning of the fifteenth century. Carols continue to be plentiful for the next hundred years after Awdlay's time. They are to be found scattered through numerous manuscripts. Two considerable gatherings of them are set as part-songs for two or three voices in music-books of the Dunstable school. At the end of the fifteenth century they still form the principal element in another collection, curiously like that of the Sloane manuscript after an interval of at least fifty years, which is now in the Bodleian. About 1524 Richard Hill, a London tradesman, brought a number of them together, with much other poetry both secular and religious from literary sources, in his commonplace book. Skelton and the musicians of Henry the Eighth's court occasionally wrote and set them; and printed books of *Christmas Carolles*, of which fragments only survive, were produced by the London stationers until well into Elizabeth's reign. It is interesting to find Awdlay's poems enduring, not only in both the song-books, but also in Richard Hill's miscellany. Most of the best carols are, however, anonymous, and the vast compilation made by the Franciscan James Ryman about 1494 chiefly serves to show how savourless a thing popular poetry can become in the adapting hands of a pious and unimaginative ecclesiastic. If Ryman is interesting at all, it is only as continuing the old Franciscan tradition of religious minstrelsy. Awdlay himself has a special devotion to St Francis, but the abbey of Haghmon, in which he wrote, was an Augustinian and not a Minorite house.

Thomas Wright, who first edited the Sloane and Bodleian manuscripts, regarded them as the professional repertories of minstrels; and indeed there is a specious air of minstrelsy about their frequent appeals to the 'more and lasse' and the 'lordings' present in hall and bower. But while they contain a small proportion of secular, satirical, and even improper pieces, their general tone is far too uniformly didactic and religious to be at all characteristic of minstrelsy. These qualities and the Latin tags with which they abound inevitably suggest that the authors were clerks, although, likely enough, clerks of the errant persuasion. Some of the Latin verses, indeed, belong definitely to the Goliardic cycle. Even John Awdlay leaves the impression of looking back on a misspent youth. And the addresses to the 'lordings' are obviously capable of another explanation. They may be those not of minstrels, but of wassailing neighbours who make their rounds at Christmastide to drink a cup and take a gift and bring good fortune upon the house. It is not necessary to labour here the folk character of a custom which, like the kindred ritual of mumming or mask, has its origin in the sacrificial perambulations of pagan festival.[1] The earliest *noëls* were no doubt wassailing songs. In an Anglo-

---

[1] Cf. *Mediæval Stage*, I, 253, 400.

Norman one of the thirteenth century, the singers hail the 'seignors' of the 'hostel' which they visit, and announce that they have come 'pur quere Noël', who, as they understand, holds his yearly revel there. The song has its burden—

> Deu doint à tuz icels joie d'amurs,
> Qui à danz Noël ferunt honors.

But in the last stanza this is varied, and two English words introduced—

> Si jo vus di trestoz *Wesseyl!*
> Dehaiz eit qui ne dirra *Drincheyl!*
>
> (Wright, *S.C.C.* i.)

The English carols of the fifteenth century do not wholly miss the festive note. There are carols of 'my lord sire Cristëmasse', or of 'Yole, thou mery man', carols of the wassail and the boar's head, carols of the contest of holly and ivy, which seems to symbolise some ancient opposition of the sexes in the folk festival. It is easy to understand how the religious element in Christmas at last prevailed and gave its own colouring to the majority of the ditties. But the religious element is the superadded and not the primitive one. The very name of carol is significant; for here, no less than in the amorous *caroles* of twelfth-century France, are represented the mingled dance and song of the village *chorus*, hailing with rhythmic exultation the coming of the summer or the winter holiday. An interesting confirmation of this relationship is afforded by the metrical structure of the carols. Their form varies considerably, but the commonest type of all, to which almost precisely half the examples in the two earliest manuscripts belong, consists of a triplet upon a single rhyme, followed by a *cauda* which is linked by a second rhyme to one or more lines of the burden. Exactly the same arrangement is to be found in several twelfth- or thirteenth-century French *caroles*, including that quoted on page 60. It is an intermediate stage between the elaborated *rondel* and the simpler scheme of the *chanson d'histoire*, in which a monorhymed *couplet*, originally perhaps of a single line, is followed by a *refrain* upon another rhyme, without any connecting link. It lends itself admirably to the methods of a dance-song shared between a leader and a *chorus*, since the change of rhyme in the *cauda* serves literally as a cue to the *chorus* that it is their turn to break in with the burden. Sometimes the whole of the *cauda*, and not merely its rhyme, is repeated from stanza to stanza, and it becomes in effect a second or inner burden. The burden or 'fote' itself remains a characteristic of the carols, long after both the dance accompaniment and the strict division of lines between a leader and a *chorus* have been forgotten.

Space fails for any sufficient analysis of the literary quality of the carols. The contrast which they present to the more ecclesiastical modes of mediæval religious poetry is remarkable. The Anglo-Saxon pessimism, the oppression of imminent mortality, the brooding sense of personal sin, pass into the background, if they do not altogether disappear. These singers approach their religious themes with something of the light-hearted simplicity of the first shepherds. They greet the coming of a Saviour without trepidation, as a gay and wonderful event.

> Mary is quene of allé thinge,
> And her sone a lovely kinge,

they chant; or with an even more naive blending of familiarity and awe—

> Blessèd be God this game is begonne,
> And his moder emperesse of helle.

Even the thought of the sin of Adam leads to its *Deo gracias*. All is for the best—

> Ne hadde the appil také ben,
> The appil taken ben,
> Ne haddé never our lady
> A ben hevené quene.

Philosophic contemplation puts on the gnomic manner of the folk. The garnered wisdom of life is summed up in proverbial phrases of unassailable homespun—

> For there is none but one of two,
> Heven to gete or heven forgo;
> Oder mene none there is.

Or again—

> Now is joye and now is bliss;
> Now is balle and bitternesse;
> Now it is and now it nis;
> Thus paseth this world away.

The world, indeed, is 'but a chery ffayre', in the

pretty metaphor of the Shropshire orchards; and the poets are content to take it for granted and to make the best of it, without repining. As compared with the ecclesiastical verse, again, the carols are markedly objective and pictorial in their apprehension of things. They are the lyric counterpart of the miracle plays; and probably they betray the actual influence of the constant visualisation of biblical scenes and personages in the periodical representations of Nativity or of Passion. Those who sang them and those who listened had looked on 'Bethlem, that faier borow' and on 'Herowd, that mody king' and the 'three kinges of great noblay', Caspar, Melchior, and Balthasar, marching in each one with his train. They could recall how Gabriel 'sat on knee, and seide *Ave!*' and how Mary 'stod stille as ony ston', and how the 'angeles cam out of here toure' to behold, clustering no doubt upon a flight of steps, as one sees them in Jean Fouquet's miniature of the *Miracle of St Apollonia*. In the carols, as in the miracle plays, the personality of the Virgin is hung about with a tender humanity. There is a series of lullabies, some of which contain dialogues between the Mother and Child comparable to those later dialogues at the Crucifixion, which are a recognised variety of the *Planctus Mariae*. To trace the development of these lullabies and their relation to the lullaby of a purely human mother in the Anglo-Irish manuscript of the early fourteenth century would be in itself a tempting theme.

## Some Aspects of Mediæval Lyric

Like the love-songs of the *chanson populaire*, the carols are not wholly of the folk, nor is the folk wholly forgotten in them. They bring up an image of the spacious coloured burgess life of which they formed a part. The flames of the Yule-log flicker upon the hearth, and the roasted crab bobs in the wassail-bowl of spiced ale. The skin-clad mummers, with their grotesque fool, have but just left the hall. Already the chanted question comes nearer and nearer along the crooked mediæval street—

> What tithingis bringst us, messangere,
> Of Cristès birth this new eris day?

And the clear voices peal out the exultant answer to the tingling stars—

> Suche wonder tithingis ye mow here,
> That maydon and modur is won i fere,
> And lady is of hye aray.

Even so 'as he lay seke in his langure' had John the blind Awdlay written it for his countrymen, in the quiet dormitory of his 'abbay here be west'.

# SIR THOMAS WYATT

THE poetry of the fifteenth century, when it is poetry, derives from folk or ecclesiastical origins, and reaches us mainly through minstrel hands. A court poetry, which had grown up with Chaucer, wilted in the hurly-burly of the Roses. And when the Tudors came, the energies of their first king, austere if not already a little world-wearied, were too closely bent upon the establishment of a dynasty and the reconstruction of a national life, to have much room for the development of that leisurely social atmosphere in which the Muses and the Graces flourish. Erasmus and Colet and the rest brought theological and classical learning, and a spirit of scholarship was abroad. But vernacular poetry only followed slowly in the wake, at the advent of a younger and more ardent Henry and a Catharine of Aragon, upon whom the shadow of Our Lady of Sorrows had not yet fallen. The migratory habit of mediæval sovereigns, itself not propitious to letters, was now abandoned, and Westminster, with its satellite palaces of Greenwich and Richmond, became the setting for that round of spectacular revelry, of which the pages of the chronicler Edward Halle furnish so vivid a record. Catharine, worn early with the burden of ineffective child-bearing, soon dropped out. But Henry's lights of love were at hand to take her place. Pageant trod hard upon pageant, and

Maying upon Maying, and the introduction of the Italian fashion of the Mask provided its abundant opportunities for the whispers that mean sometimes less and sometimes more than they seem to mean. In such an environment the encounter of bright eyes and warm bloods found its natural outcome in amorous versifying. Music, of which there had long been a tradition in the English court, lent its aid; and the simpler patterns of melody devised by the lutenists made a suitable background for lyrical utterance. But the making of 'balettes' was by no means left to such professional exponents of the art as William Cornish of the Chapel Royal and John Heywood. Henry himself made them, and it was the last nail in the coffin of Anne Boleyn that she turned his attempts to derision.[1] The courtiers took up the fashion; Anne's brother Lord Rochford, Thomas Lord Vaux, Lord Thomas Howard, Sir Francis Bryan, Sir Anthony Lee. They are little more than names to us, and most of their contributions, if they have survived at all, are presumably buried in the 'Poems by Uncertain Authors', which form part of the *Songes and Sonettes* published by Richard Tottel in 1557. But in the forefront of the singing company stands Sir Thomas Wyatt. He, too, is in Tottel, but apart from the anonymous crowd. Here, indeed, he takes second place to Henry Howard, Earl of Surrey, who was of a younger generation. But to his initiative, in the eyes of his

[1] *Calendar of Spanish Papers*, v (2), 128.

contemporaries, the *Naeniae* of the antiquary John
Leland on his tomb bear sufficient testimony.

Anglica lingua fuit rudis, et sine nomine rhythmus:
Nunc limam agnoscit, docte Viate, tuam;

and again—

Nobilitas didicit, te praeceptore, Britanna,
Carmina per varios scribere posse modos.

Of Wyatt's career, apart from what bears upon
his poetry, I will only give a bare outline. He
belonged to one of the new families which came to
dignity under the Tudors through direct service to
the crown, and acquired wealth, not so much from
official emoluments as from royal grants of escheated lands, and at a later date from the acquisi-
tion on easy terms of those reft from monasteries.
Less conservative than the older nobility, with
whom, however, they often intermarried, they
eagerly adopted the new learning, and were often
touched by Lutheran tendencies. Sir Henry
Wyatt, the father of Thomas, had suffered imprisonment as a Lancastrian under Richard the
Third. He became a privy councillor to Henry the
Seventh and his son, and held the important household post of Treasurer of the Chamber. His chief
estate was at Allington Castle in Kent. Thomas,
who spelt his own name Wiat, was born in 1503
and educated at St John's College, Cambridge.
About 1520 he married Elizabeth, the daughter of
Thomas Brooke, Lord Cobham, and had by her a
son, also a Thomas, who afterwards brought the

family fortunes to ruin in a Protestant rising
against Queen Mary. Elizabeth proved unfaithful,
was repudiated by her husband about 1526 and
probably never forgiven. Thomas's sister Margaret
married his fellow-poet Sir Anthony Lee. Thomas
was at court, helping in his father's financial duties,
by 1523, and in 1524, being then an Esquire of
the Body, received the post of Clerk of the King's
Jewels. Edward Halle notes him as one of the
challengers in a feat of arms at the Christmas of
1525. In 1526 he entered upon the career of
diplomacy which was to occupy much of his life, in
the train of Sir Thomas Cheyne as ambassador to
Paris, and displayed, according to Cheyne's report,
'as much wit to remember and remark every thing
he seeth as any young man hath in England'. In
1527 he similarly went with Sir John Russell to
Rome, and had the misfortune to be captured
during a pleasure trip to Ferrara by imperial troops
and the adroitness to escape while negotiations for
his release were in progress. For Catharine he
translated Plutarch's *Quyete of Mynde*, through the
Latin, as a gift at the new year of 1528, having
quailed before the longer task of Petrarch's *De
Remediis utriusque Fortunae*.[1] From some date in
1528 to November 1530 he was absent from court
as High Marshal of Calais. In June 1533 he was
deputy for his father as Chief Ewer at the coro-
nation of Anne Boleyn. May 1534 saw him in the
Fleet as the result of an affray with the sergeants of

[1] Ed. C. R. Baskervill (1931).

London, in which one of them was slain. But a greater misadventure yet was to befall him. The arrest of Anne Boleyn for the high treason of infidelity to the king on May 1, 1536, was followed on May 5 by that of Wyatt. To this I shall have to return. But that Wyatt had not fundamentally lost the royal confidence is shown by his release some six weeks later, by his appointment in the following summer to military duties about the king's person during the northern rebellion, by the selection of him as Sheriff of Kent in November, and even more notably by his despatch in the following spring as ambassador to the Emperor Charles the Fifth in Spain. On his departure he was knighted and a year or so later made a Gentleman of the Privy Chamber. The death of his father towards the end of 1536 had left him the head of his family, and from Spain he wrote two letters of counsel to his son, the younger Thomas, which are full of good feeling and a ripe wisdom of life. His theme is Honesty.

And here I call not honesty that men commonly call honesty, as reputation for riches, for authority, or some like thing, but that honesty, that I dare well say your Grandfather (whose soul God pardon) had rather left to me than all the lands he did leave me; that was wisdom, gentleness, soberness, desire to do good, friendliness to get the love of many, and truth above all the rest. A great part to have all these things is to desire to have them, and although Glory and honest name are not the very end wherefore these things are to be followed, yet surely they must needs follow them as light followeth fire, though it were kindled for warmth.

Wyatt's mission fell at one of many critical moments in the shifting triangular relations between England, France and the Empire. His main charge was to keep Charles the Fifth in play with negotiations for marriages between Henry and Christina of Milan and between the Princess Mary and the Infant of Portugal; and thereby to ward off a threatened understanding between the Emperor and Francis the First, which would leave his king in a state of isolation and exposed to the dangers of a General Council desired by the Pope. In this he was not successful, mainly, as he seems to have thought, because Henry himself fumbled, when a chance of securing his object arose. But his accomplishments and in particular a gift of witty discourse, of which the samples that have come down to us seem rather to have lost their glitter, made him a *persona grata* with the Emperor, and inspired alarm among the papal agents. Their attempts to counteract his influence took shape in an accusation of disseminating heretical writings in Spain, and Charles, as Wyatt himself tells us, had much ado to save him from the embraces of the Inquisition. There were enemies, too, in his own country, who worked on very different lines. Among much official correspondence about the embassy are preserved some personal letters between Wyatt and Thomas Cromwell, then at the height of his power. They show the minister in an unusually favourable light. There is clearly a bond of friendship between him and Wyatt. He does his best to guide the steps of a diplomatist who is still something of a novice, occasionally reproving him for small irregularities, but careful also to commend his industry and dexterity, and to pass on any favourable reception of his despatches by the King. And he has charged himself, during Wyatt's absence, with the oversight of his private affairs, which he found 'but rawly left', and showing signs both of carelessness in business transactions and of undue generosity in making loans to others. But Cromwell did not trust any man all the way, and Wyatt was later to receive the impression that he had been put under the observation of Thomas Bonner, who was sent to join him in Spain, as a canonist able to expound Henry's objections to a General Council. However this may be, the pushing and ill-conditioned priest proved an uncongenial colleague for Wyatt, and on leaving Spain began to approach Cromwell with insinuating letters in which, while professing admiration for the ambassador's good qualities, he piled up charges against him; of disrespect for himself, of failure to back up his special mission, of loose living among the Spanish nuns, and of disloyal speeches about his sovereign. Wyatt, he suggests, was too much under the influence of his secretary John Mason, 'as very a papist as any I know', whom Bonner believed to be in correspondence with the traitor Reginald Pole.[1] He does not, so far as extant letters go,

[1] *Letters and Papers of the Reign of Henry VIII* (R.O.), xiii (2), 57, 107, 237.

openly implicate Wyatt in this, but one can hardly doubt his responsibility for the story noised in England about this time, that the ambassador was 'run away to the Bishop of Rome'. Cromwell, of course, knew better, but Mason was imprisoned and examined, and succeeded in clearing himself and Wyatt. News of the 'suspect' into which he had fallen reached Wyatt in Spain, and he wrote to Cromwell, asking for his recall, that he might give an account of himself. It was not granted, but when he did return in April 1539, Cromwell was able to assure him that the matter was satisfactorily at rest. Later in the year, Wyatt was sent on a second embassy to the Emperor, whom he accompanied on a visit to Paris and afterwards to Flanders. And at Paris he certainly scored a diplomatic triumph, leading Charles by a charge of ingratitude towards Henry into an assertion of superiority over all other sovereigns, which was capable of effective use in sowing mistrust between him and Francis. Wyatt's vivacious account of the interview provides better reading than is common in ambassadorial despatches. When he once more reached England about April 1540, Cromwell was already tottering to his fall. Wyatt was present at the execution on July 28, and Cromwell bade him not to weep, 'for if I were no more guilty than thou wert when they took thee, I should not now be in this pass'.[1] It was a last act of friendship, and an

[1] M. A. S. Hume, *Chronicle of Henry VIII in Spanish*, 104.

ineffective one. It was not long before Bonner, now
in enjoyment of the bishopric of London, which
he was one day to incarnadine, renewed his attack
upon Wyatt, and on this occasion the old grievances were made to culminate in a definite accusation of practising with the Cardinal. It was taken
seriously. Wyatt was again sent to the Tower, and
from here he composed a letter to the Privy Council
and a speech to his judges, which have come down
to us. They read convincingly enough. He asserts
his complete loyalty to Henry and his arduous
services in an embassy unwillingly undertaken, 'for
that I was given to a more pleasant kind of life'.
He admits some indiscretions in his references to
his former imprisonment and to the king's dis-
comfiture between Charles and Francis. He is
'wont sometime to rap out an oath in an earnest
talk', and might have said 'By God's blood, the
King is left out of the cart's tail'. But he denies
the interpretation that had been put upon his
words. That he has no papalist tendencies is no-
torious. He had done no offence with nuns. 'I
grant I do not profess chastity; but yet I use not
abomination.' Mason had certainly been in communication with Pole, at the instigation of Bonner
as well as himself, but solely for the purpose of
trying to worm secrets out of him. It was a
common practice of all ambassadors within their
discretion. The attempt, which was unsuccessful,
was reported to Cromwell at the time. And upon
Bonner himself, his pompousness, his lack of dig-

nity, his disregard of religious observances, his own
ethical lapses, although he, as a priest, had professed chastity, Wyatt retorts with scathing irony.
We have no full report of the trial. Wyatt, however, was released after three months' imprisonment. Officially it was stated that he had confessed
and had been pardoned at the intercession of
Queen Catharine Howard.[1] The Spanish ambassador had been told of a condition that he must
take back his wife, with whose sister Henry
became intimate.[2] However this may be, it is
clear that the growing suspiciousness of Henry's
later years did not bear hard upon Wyatt. He was
given a command of light horse at Calais, and a
year later nominated to the vice-admiralship of a
fleet in preparation.[3] But death intervened. An
envoy from the Emperor reached Falmouth in
October 1542. Wyatt was deputed to meet him and
bring him to London. Riding hard, he fell into
a fever, and was tended by Sir John Horsey of
Clifton Maubank, in whose vault at Sherborne he
lies.

One may infer that the 'more pleasant kind of
life', which Wyatt so reluctantly abandoned at the
call of public duty, was very much that of a cultivated English gentleman in all ages. In trouble,
he thinks of 'Luckes my faire falcon and your
fellowes all' as his chief friends. In retirement,

[1] *L.P.* xvi, 314, 318, 329.
[2] *L.P.* xvi, 319; xvii, 717.
[3] *L.P.* xvi, 339; xvii, 341, 742.

quit of court with its *tracasseries* and the burden of foreign travel, he tells John Poynz,

> A chipp of chaunce more than a pownd of witt.
> This maketh me at home to hounte and to hawke,
> And in fowle weder at my booke to sitt;
>
> In frost and snowe then with my bow to stawke;
> No man doeth marke where so I ride or goo;
> In lusty lees at libertie I walke.

And much of the pleasantness, no doubt, lay in his gift of verse-making.

> Here I ame in Kent and Christendome,
> Emong the muses where I rede and ryme.

Probably many of Wyatt's poems passed from hand to hand during his life-time. They are preserved, sporadically or in bulk, by half-a-dozen manuscripts, some of which are not strictly contemporary. For several of these we have to thank John Harington (*c.* 1520–82) and his son Sir John Harington (*c.* 1561–1612), both of whom were themselves poets. The most important collections are Additional MS. 17492, known as the Devonshire MS., and Egerton MS. 2711. So far as the substance of the poems is concerned, the Devonshire MS. appears to be the earlier of the two. It is written in diverse hands, and bears on its title-page or elsewhere the names of Henry's bastard the Duke of Richmond, and his wife Mary Howard, of Mary's brother the Earl of Surrey, of Margaret Douglas, who married firstly Lord Thomas

Howard and secondly the Earl of Lennox, and of
Mary Shelton, who may have been a sister of Anne
Boleyn's maid of honour and Henry's favourite,
Margaret Shelton. Wyatt's pieces predominate,
although some, which have been ascribed to him
by conjecture, must remain uncertain. But among
them are interspersed contributions by various
writers, several of whom are not otherwise known;
the Earl of Surrey himself, Thomas Howard, Sir
Anthony Lee, Edmund Knyvett, Richard Hatfield, C. Lanselles, an anonymous A.I. or A.J. A
single poem, by Henry Stewart, Earl of Darnley,
the ill-fated husband of Mary Queen of Scots,
must be a later addition. The book is likely to have
belonged to some member of the Howard family.
Wyatt's recent editor, Miss Foxwell, has construc-
ted an ingenious romance, parts of which may be
true, in which it is successively transferred from
Wyatt or his father to Surrey, from him to his
sister and Richmond on their marriage in 1533,
from the Duchess to Lady Lennox, from her to
her son Darnley, from Darnley to Mary of Scots,
and from her to the Earl and Countess of Shrews-
bury, from whose house of Chatsworth it came.
The Egerton MS. is of Harington *provenance*. It
contains some of the poems found in the Devonshire MS., together with many others. A few,
towards the end, were written out by Wyatt himself. The greater number are in a single scribal
hand, but Wyatt has gone over them, making
textual alterations, setting his initials in the margin,

and indicating a classification into five groups, of short lyrics, sonnets, odes, psalms and satires respectively. His revision, of course, gives this manuscript a primary textual authority, and it is notable that some of the wording which he corrected in it appears in its original form in the Devonshire MS. It must be added that, in spite of Wyatt's pains, the Egerton MS. by no means gives a perfect text. Both here and in the Devonshire MS. many words have obviously been misread, and many others, necessary to the sense or the metre, have been omitted. Editors have proved unduly timid in exercising their right and obligation of conjectural emendation in such cases, and Wyatt's plain meaning has often been obscured. A third substantial collection, used by G. F. Nott in his edition of 1816, is now only known through a modern transcript in Additional MS. 28635, but other contents of this show that the original cannot have been of earlier date than the time of Sir John Harington. Small additions to the canon are made by this and by Harleian MS. 78 and C.C.C.C. MS. 168. But Additional MS. 36529, also a Harington manuscript of the late sixteenth century, only yields textual variants.

Wyatt's handling of the Egerton MS. suggests that he meant to publish his poems, and this is confirmed by some lines in the Devonshire MS., which have all the appearance of an *Envoi*. They end as follows:

And patientely, O reader, I the praye,
  Take in good parte this worke as yt ys mente,
And greve thee not with ought that I shalle saye,
  Sins with good will this boke abrode ys sente,
To tell men howe in youthe I ded assaye
  What love ded mene, and nowe I yt repente,
    That musing me my frendes might well be ware,
    And kepe them free from all such payne and care.[1]

There is no evidence and small probability that he ever carried out this design. But some of his poems, in texts for which he can hardly be responsible, found their way into printed books, other than Tottel's. They only survive in fragments, and in these Wyatt's name does not appear. The longest fragment, formerly at Britwell, is now in the Folger Library at Washington. It consists of one octavo sheet, forming the beginning of a volume. I give the contents in an Appendix. A title-page runs, 'The Courte of Venus. Newly and diligently corrected with many proper Ballades newly amended, and also added thervnto which haue not before bene imprinted'. A Prologue, in halting rhyme royal, tells of Venus, of a hapless lover who would learn the fashion of her court, and of Genius who gives him counsel. The personages must derive ultimately from Gower's *Confessio Amantis*. The opening is—

In the moneth of may when the new tender grene
Hath smothly couered the ground that was bare.

[1] Devonshire has 'Yet moving' in l. 7. I have ventured to emend.

III

At the close of this is the note, 'Thus endeth the prologue, and hereafter foloweth the new court of Venus'. Then come eleven songs and the first stanza of a twelfth, with which the fragment breaks off. Of the eleven, five are Wyatt's. A sixth ('Loue whom you lyst and spare not') is an elaboration of lines by him in the Devonshire MS. Of the rest one can only say that, while in various degrees they suggest Wyatt's phrasing and love for a refrain, the presence of his controlling mind is less obvious. It is difficult to distinguish, especially through bad texts, between a great poet, not at his greatest, and a smaller man under his influence. The Folger fragment was almost certainly printed by Thomas Marsh about 1561–65. But another, Bodleian Douce g. 3, cannot, in view of its pagination and typography, have come from the same volume. It consists of two sheets, also from a small octavo. Here are the end of one song and the whole of another ('Dryuen by dissyr to set affection'), which again has echoes of lines by Wyatt in the Devonshire MS. These are followed by *The Pilgrim's Tale*, which is an anti-ecclesiastical satire, with the opening—

> In Lincolneshyr, fast by the fene,
> ther stant a hows, and you yt ken.

A third fragment has only been recently discovered in the form of two leaves used as end papers to a copy of Ralph Robinson's translation (1551) from More's *Utopia* in the library of the University

of Texas.[1] The leaves are continuous, and the first
is numbered 44. The running-title is *A Boke of
Balettes*. Here, a good deal mutilated, are five
poems, all of which are also traceable in the Folger
fragment of *The Court of Venus*. Three are Wyatt's,
a fourth is again 'Loue whom you lyst and spare
not', and the fifth is a complete form of the broken
piece which ends the Folger fragment. The agreement in content seems to indicate a relationship
between the *Boke* and the *Court*. A comparison of
their texts, moreover, shows that, subject to minor
variants, they represent the same versions, which
are not those of the Wyatt manuscripts for the
poems therein contained. Here the *Boke* and there
the *Court* gives the better reading of a line. Both
have a habit of omitting necessary words. And
neither is good enough to make Wyatt's own oversight at all plausible.

The existence of *A Boke of Balettes* further
complicates a bibliographical problem which was
already difficult.[2] The *Stationers' Register*, half way
through a list of copyright allowances from July
1557 to July 1558, has the entry, 'To Henry
Sutton, to prynte this booke, Called the Couurte of

[1] R. H. Griffith and R. A. Law, *A Boke of Balettes and The
Courte of Venus* (1930, *Univ. of Texas Studies in English*, 10);
cf. *Times Literary Supplement* for July 5 and 12, 1928,
December 26, 1929, and September 4, 1930.

[2] F. J. Furnivall, *Animadversions of Francis Thynne* (2 *Chaucer
Soc.* XIII, pp. xlvi, 8, 77, 127, 138); C. C. Stopes, *Shakespeare's
Industry* (1916), 305; A. W. Foxwell, *Poems of Sir Thomas
Wiat*, II, 171.

Venus, and for his lycense he geveth to the howse iiij<sup>d</sup>'.[1] The Douce fragment may be earlier than Sutton. Clearly there was more than one edition of the *Court*. The title-page and the note after the Prologue show that the Folger fragment cannot belong to the first. And there is evidence that in some form a *Court of Venus* existed a good many years before 1558. Towards the end of the *Pilgrim's Tale*, the author claims that 'vi stavis' which follow are 'Chaucer's own hand wark'. This probably explains why John Bale in his *Scriptores* of 1548 includes in a list of Chaucer's writings—

De Curia Veneris. li. i. In Maio cum virescerent, etc., and elsewhere in the list—
Narrationes Diversorum. trac. i. In Comitatu Lyncolniensi fuit, etc.

He was of course in error. But his Latin is based on the opening lines of the Folger Prologue and the Douce *Pilgrim's Tale*. It seems possible that he had seen or heard of the two pieces, in manuscript or print, together. And they may have been in circulation as early as 1540, if it is rightly supposed that Bale possessed the material for his *Scriptores* when he left England in that year, not to return until 1548, when it was printed. Later Bale seems, for a time, to have recognised his error. In some notes begun about 1549, he puts neither poem under Chaucer's name, and says no more of the *Pilgrim's Tale*, unless he means to include it in a

[1] Arber, I, 78.

*Curia Veneris,* which he here gives to one Robert Shyngleton, a priest who *patiebatur* in 1544.[1] On the other hand, the *Scriptores* of 1557–9 revert to the Chaucerian attributions of 1548, and although Shyngleton is here, he only gets theological works, with the added biographical details that he recanted in 1543 and was said to have been hanged at London *inter proditionis reos* in 1544. We gather a little of Robert Shyngleton or Singleton from other sources. He had been a chaplain to Anne Boleyn. His recantation, with those of two better known heretics, Thomas Becon and Robert Wisdom, took place at Paul's Cross on 8 July 1543, when he declared himself 'an unlearned fantastical fool' and tore up his writings. Bishop Gardiner mentions his conspiracy in a letter of 1547.[2] Robert Singleton might well have written the anti-ecclesiastical *Pilgrim's Tale,* which cannot be of earlier date than 1536, since it mentions as a recent rebel 'owr cobler the dawe', who is doubtless the 'Captain Cobler' recorded by Holinshed as a leader in the Lincolnshire rising of that year. There is nothing in the Prologue to suggest that it is likely to have come from the same hand as the *Tale.* But in any case, we cannot credit a militant Protestant with the composition of amorous ditties, the presence of which in a *Court of Venus* made it an early mark for the reprobation of a long succession of moralists,

[1] *Index Scriptorum* (ed. R. L. Poole), 389.
[2] *L.P.* xviii (1), 313; J. Gairdner, *Lollardy and the Reformation in England,* ii, 380.

belonging to Singleton's own school, and including
that very Thomas Becon who recanted with him in
1543.[1] The first of those critics seems to have been
John Hall, who has several allusions to the *Court*
in the preface to *Certain Chapters of the Proverbes
Translated into Metre* (1550). Thus he wishes 'the
gyggolot gerles were as well learned in virtue and
godliness as they be in yᵉ Court of Venus'. And he
thinks that spiritual versifiers 'have as moche de-
served to be commended as he, whatsoever he was,
that made yᵉ Court of Venus, or other bokes of
lecherous Ballades'. We may perhaps find other
qualities in Wyatt's verse now, without re-opening
one of the oldest of literary controversies. Hall's
wording here suggests that he did not know the
authorship of the *Court*. In his later *Courte of
Vertu* (1565) which was itself printed, with pleasing
indifference to the controversy, by Thomas Marsh,
he returns to the charge.

> A booke also of songes they have,
>     And Venus court they doe it name;
> No filthy mynde a songe can crave,
>     But therin he may finde the same:
>     And in such songes is all their game.
>         Whereof ryght dyuers bookes be made,
>         To nuryshe that most fylthy trade.

And it is interesting to observe that among his own
'Ballettes' in this volume, three are spiritual parodies
of Wyatt's 'My lute, awake', 'My pen, take pain',
and 'Blame not my lute', of which the first two are

---

[1] Stopes, *ut supra*, 305.

in the Folger fragment of the *Court* and the first only is in Tottel. Becon's similar attack on the *Court* as a 'filthy' book is in his *Booke of Matrimony*, which first appears in his *Worckes* of 1564 and has an Elizabethan Epistle. The *Worckes* were registered in 1560 and the *Matrimony* may have been written still earlier. At any rate Becon does not appear conscious that one of the contributors to the 'filthy' book was the Sir Thomas Wyatt to whom he had dedicated his *New Pollecye of Warre* in 1542, as being one who had 'embrased not only the studies of humaine letters, but also the grave exercises of divine literature'. No doubt Wyatt, being something of a Protestant, as well as an amorist, presented a critical problem to his serious-minded contemporaries.

And now one may perhaps sketch a possible history as follows. A *Pilgrim's Tale* and a *Court of Venus*, wrongly believed by him to be by the same author, were known to Bale, perhaps only in manuscript. If either of them was by Singleton, it is not likely to have been printed during 1540–6, or at any rate 1543–6. But, if not before 1540, then in Edward's reign, by 1550, both pieces were put into a book, and accompanied by some balettes. To these the *Court* served as a prologue. It also gave a title to the book. Either in the first or in a subsequent edition, some of Wyatt's floating pieces were included. They may have been first gathered for an independent *Boke of Balettes*, and taken for the *Court* from that. They remained anonymous, and were not picked up by Tottel, who drew from other sources. But the appearance of Tottel led to a registration of the *Court* by Sutton. He may have printed it, but the Folger fragment belongs to a new edition by Thomas Marsh some years later. The Douce fragment was thought by Furnivall, on the evidence of dropped lines and misprinted words, to be also part of a reprint, but this does not seem to me quite conclusive. Tottel's own collection was probably on a larger scale. He gives a block of ninety-one poems and adds six more in an appendix. There are a few which are not preserved elsewhere. He may have had the use of a comprehensive and fairly authoritative manuscript. If so, it was not one of those known to us. Occasionally his text seems to furnish a legitimate correction to theirs. Conceivably his editor, supposed to be Nicholas Grimald, was capable of some sound conjectural emendations. But one must give the preference, wherever possible, to Wyatt's own Egerton MS., and after that, with less confidence, to the Devonshire MS. For undoubtedly Tottel's text has undergone sophistication. Wyatt's language has certain constant features. Thus he often elides the *e* in the inflection *-eth*, making monosyllables, for example, of such words as *loveth*, *flyeth*, *helpeth*. On the other hand he sometimes preserves the earlier sounded *e* of plural and genitive forms in *-es*, such as *eyès*, *lovès*. He gives a Romance accent to many words of French or Latin origin. It seems clear that, within comparatively few years after his death, such habits had come to be regarded as archaisms, and were eliminated by the editor or the transcriber of his manuscript. Moreover, the sophisticator failed to appreciate Wyatt's free syllabic handling of iambic metres; the ready substitution of an anapaest in any foot, the occasional trochees, the frequent omission of an unstressed syllable, generally in the first foot. All lines so affected he tended to reduce to a regular iambic norm, and much delicacy of rhythm vanished. It must be added that Wyatt's poems, like others in the *Songes and Sonettes*, were fitted by the editor with fanciful titles to his own taste.

About a hundred and twenty of the poems, gathered from all sources, may be classed as lyrical 'balettes'. We need not assume that they were all in fact set to music, for which some of them are rather long. But constant references to singing and the lute sufficiently indicate the origin of the *genre*. The range of metrical variation is very wide; more than seventy distinct stanza-forms are to be found in the hundred and twenty examples. The basis is nearly always iambic. Pentameters, tetrameters, trimeters, dimeters are all used, separately and in combination, in mono-rhyme and in cross-rhyme, with and without refrains. The types are those known in the neo-Latin poetry of the *vagantes* and analysed in mediæval treatises on poetics.[1] Many of them also appear in earlier vernacular poetry. Here

[1] Cf. J. M. Berdan, *Early Tudor Poetry* (1931), 120 *sqq.*

Wyatt is at the end rather than the beginning of a tradition. He handles it as a master, with a facility of rhythmical accomplishment to which his Elizabethan successors, although they had many qualities which he had not, rarely attained.

> Whom speke I to,
> Unkynd and deff of ere;
> Alas, lo, I go,
> And wot not where.
>
> Where is my thoght?
> Where wanders my desire?
> Where may the thing be soght,
> That I require?
>
> Light in the wynde
> Doth fle all my delight;
> Where trouth and faithfull mynde
> Are put to flyght.
>
> Who shall me gyve
> Fethered wynges for to fle,
> The thing that doeth me greve
> That I may se?

What a delicate art determined the interchange of rhyme between the short and longer lines here, and how subtly the overflows of sense are managed.

Side by side with the balettes, there are a number of pieces in metres of foreign origin, the sonnet, ottava rima and terza rima of Italy, the rondeau of France, together with a few of some length in the English rhyme-royal and the 'poulter's measure'. And in many, although not all, of these the substance is based upon Italian or French, or in a few cases Latin, models. Wyatt's reading has a fair scope, but the authors most commonly drawn upon are Petrarch, Serafino De' Ciminelli dall' Aquila and Clément Marot. The measure of indebtedness varies from very close translation to the loosest of paraphrase. This division of Wyatt's work furnishes something of a puzzle. Much of it, especially in the sonnets, is stiff and difficult to scan; and even when full allowance has been made, both for Romance accentuation and for textual corruption, many lines can only be regarded as simply unmetrical. The contrast with the finished *technique* of the balettes is very striking. Attempts have been made to explain these derivative poems as prentice-work, in which Wyatt was fumbling his way to a comprehension of the pentameter, with the help of a text of Chaucer perverted by oblivion of the Chaucerian inflections. I cannot say that I find them plausible. No doubt Wyatt read Chaucer, and no doubt the true Chaucerian line had long been lost and the versions current in the sixteenth century lent themselves to misinterpretation. But Wyatt, in the balettes, shows himself as finished a craftsman with the pentameter as with any other measure. Clearly he understood it when they were written, and there is no reason for ascribing a priority in time to the sonnets and their congeners. Apart from a few individual pieces which can be linked to Wyatt's life, there is no material for a chronology. Certainly it cannot be assumed, as Miss Foxwell appears to assume, that the order of the Egerton MS. is an order of composition. A period of Italian influence has been sought in the fleeting visit to Italy of 1527 and a period of French influence in the longer sojourn at Calais during 1528–30. This may be fanciful, but in any case much of the balette-making is likely to have come before. Love is predominantly an activity of youth. I cannot, of course, prove that some of the more awkward sonnets were not early. But it is noticeable, I think, that the awkwardness is at its height in those which most closely follow their originals. And my impression is that these ought to be regarded as mere exercises in translation or adaptation, roughly jotted down in whatever broken rhythms came readiest to hand, and intended perhaps for subsequent polishing at some time of leisure which never presented itself. However this may be, in a sane estimate of Wyatt's achievement, the exotic writing is of little account. It is true that a dozen historians of literature acclaim it as his chief merit that he introduced the sonnet into England. But a writer's merit lies in what he accomplishes, not in what baffles him. It is the quality of emotional expression in poetry, not its technical form, which fundamentally matters, although no doubt the form often helps to determine the quality. Our historians have seen things in the wrong perspective, betrayed by a type of scholarship which sheers away from the approach to personality in literature, and busies itself with the evolution of literary types and the transmission from writer to writer of individual literary motives and images. Source-hunting has long been the bane of academic study. It is intelligible enough. Judgements of fact are always easier than judgements of value. And the study of English, in particular, is still suffering from the past domination of continental professors, who brought to it much scientific industry, but were not unnaturally somewhat deaf to the finer felicities of an alien speech.

The balettes, too, have been diligently examined for foreign echoes. But here, if they are not altogether illusory, they rarely amount to more than a stray phrase, from Petrarch or another, which gives Wyatt a hint for independent treatment. His theme is almost invariably love, but his temper and way of approach are not always the same. Often, like Petrarch himself, he adopts the convention of bondage in love, which the whole mediæval world learnt from the troubadours of Provence. He is, and long has been his lady's 'thrall'.

> The sute, the servys, none tell can.

He is tied by

> The knot which fyrst my hert did strayn.

He can never slip it. His heart is in her hold. He sends it to her for a New Year token.

> I cannot gyve browches nor ringes,
> Thes Goldsmithes work and goodlye thinges,
>   Piery nor perle, oryente and clere;
> But for all that is no man bringes
>   Leffer Juell unto his Lady dere,
>   Dare I well say, then that I give to yere.

123

He is humble; she may do with him even as she lists.

> I have no wrong, where I can clayme no right.

But the lady is 'a cruel rebel to love'. His reward is nothing but high disdain. His words are wasted in the wind; she only turns them into mockery. He gets no response, for she has no feeling. She sends a flame from frozen breast. Like all the lovers in all the years, he burns and freezes at once. Or again, she who sends the flame sends also a shower of tears to quench it, so that it avails him nothing to terminate his pain. He suffers; he is pale and wan; he finds no rest.

> The place of slepe, wherin I do but wake,
> Bysprent with teares, my bedd I thee forsake.

The earth weeps for him; the huge oaks roar in the wind; the rivers stop their course to hear his woeful complaint. She alone has no pity. She is his foe and enjoys his pain. She is a tiger fell; a stone; you cannot grave in her. He sings like the swan,

> I dye, I dye, and you regarde yt note.

He asks for death. Nay, he is already dead, and she will not believe it.

> It is not now, but long and long ago,
> I have you served as to my powre and myght,
> As faithfully as any man might do,
> Clayming of you nothing of right, of right.
> Save of your grace only to save my liff,
> That fleith as fast as clowd afore the wynde,
> For sins that first I entred in this stryff,
> An inward deth hath fret my mynde, my mynd.

## Sir Thomas Wyatt

If I had suffred this, to you unware,
  Myn were the fawte and you nothing to blame,
But syns you know my woo and all my care,
  Why do I dy? Alas, for shame, for shame!

I know right well my face, my lowke, my teres,
  Myn Iyes, my Wordes, and eke my drery chiere,
Have cryd my deth full oft into your eres.
  Herd of belefe it doeth appere, appere.

A better prouff I se that ye would have,
  How I ame dede; therefore when ye here tell,
Beleve it not, all tho ye se my grave.
  Cruel, unkynd! I say farewell, farewell!

To all this the lover has nothing to oppose but his
constancy, and that is unshakeable.

The tyme doeth passe, yet shall not passe my love;
  Tho I be farre, alwayis my hert is nere;
Tho other chaunge, yet will I not remove;
  Tho other care not, yet love I will and fere;
Tho other hate, yet will I love my dere;
  Tho other will of lightnes saye adewe,
  Yet woll I be founde stedéfast and trewe.

And constancy brings patience. Wyatt has half a
dozen songs of which the burden is patience. And
his lute helps him.

My faithful lute
  Alone shall here me plaine,
For els all other sute
  Is clene in vaine.

This absolute self-surrender in love belongs,
once more, to the mediæval rather than the Tudor
scheme of things, wherein loves were lighter and

125

more sensuous. But the Tudor mood, too, is often Wyatt's. Fortune, who rolls her ball and turns her wheel, has sometimes favoured him. One occasion he recalls in particular, for the sweetness of it,

> When her lose gowne from her shoulders did fall,
> And she me caught in her armes long and small,
> Therewith all swetely did me kysse,
> And softely saide, 'Dere hert, howe like you this?'

But success is a fleeting joy. Fortune, who gives, will take away. Love is only a game of dice; ill luck but 'a drawght drawyn awry'. The root of the evil is in the nature of womanhood,

> that thing,
> Unstable, unsure, and wavering.

They are all for 'new fangilness'. You cannot hold them.

> I leve of therefore,
> Sins in a nett I seke to hold the wynde.

After all, a Tudor gentleman does not so easily accommodate himself to a life of unrewarded service. Patience may be proof against cruelty, but when falsehood is superadded, there comes a breaking-point.

> In faythe methynkes it is no ryght
> To hate me thus for lovyng ye;
> So fayre a face, so full of spyght,
> Who wold have thowght such crueltye.
> But syns there is no remedye,
> That by no meanes ye can me love,
> I shall you leve and other prove.

For yff I have for my good wyll
No reward eles but cruelltye,
In faythe thereoff I can no skyll
Sythe that I lovyd ye honestlye;
But take hede I wyll tyll I dye,
Or that I love so well agayn,
Syns women use so muche to fayn.

Like other disappointed amorists, Wyatt turns to palinode. Here too his lute shall help him.

Spyght askyth spyght and changing change,
And falsyd faith must nedes be knowne;
The faute so grett, the case so strange,
Of ryght it must abrode be blowne.
Then sins that by thyn own desartt
My songes do tell how trew thou artt,
Blame not my lute.

And if falsehood go with cruelty, well, he can be cruel in his turn. Some day she shall be like Villon's *belle heaulmière*, deserted, reminiscent.

Prowd of the spoyll that thou hast gott
Of simple hertes, thorough love's shot,
By whome, unkynd, thou hast theim wone,
Thinck not he hath his bow forgot,
All tho my lute and I have done.
Vengeaunce shall fall on thy disdain,
That makest but game on ernest pain;
Thinck not alone under the sonne
Unquyt to cause thy lovers plain,
All tho my lute and I have done.
Perchaunce the lye wethered and old,
The wynter nyghts that are so cold,
Playning in vain unto the mone;
Thy wisshes then dare not be told;
Care then who lyst, for I have done.

And then may chaunce the to repent
The tyme that thou hast lost and spent,
To cause thy lovers sigh and swone;
Then shalt thou knowe beaultie but lent,
And wisshe and want as I have done.

And for himself liberty is best. He has been 'tanglid in loves snare' and has escaped. He will leave the 'folish trade', and in his verse others shall read the wisdom of one that 'rotten bowes ded clyme'.

And few there ys but fyrst or last
A tyme in love ones shall they have;
And glad I am my tyme is past,
Henceforthe my fredome to withsave.
Now in my heart there shall I grave
The groundyd grace that now I tast;
Thankyd be fortune that me gave
So fayre a gyfft, so sure and fast.

And after all he proves to have been over-confident. 'Ecce deus fortior me', although he does not quote it.

A! my herte, A! what aileth the
To sett so light my libertye,
Making me bonde when I was fre?
A! my herte, A! what aileth thee?

When thou ware rid from all distresse,
Voyde of all paine and pensifnesse,
To chose againe a new mistresse,
A! my herte, A! what aileth thee?

When thou ware well, thou could not hold;
To torne agayne that ware too bold;
Thus to renue my sorowes olde,
A! my herte, A! what aileth thee?

## Sir Thomas Wyatt

Thou knoist full well that but of late
I was tornid out of lovės gate,
And now to guide me to this mate!
   A! my herte, A! what aileth thee?

I hopte full well all had ben done,
But now my hope is tane and won.
To my torment to yelde so sone,
   A! my herte, A! what aileth thee?

There is but little fundamental resemblance between Wyatt and Petrarch. He does not dwell upon the physical beauty of his lady; you learn little more than that her hair is of 'crispid gold'. He docs not couple her in proud compare of everything that is in heaven and earth; there is but one perfunctory allusion to lilies and roses. Nor of course does he, like Petrarch, veil her in that circumambient penumbra of spirituality. He makes little use of visual imagery. His range of metaphor is restricted and rather conventional. For the most part he is content with the plainest of words, and relies for his effect upon his rhythmical accomplishment. This economy of speech gives him at times a singular plangency. In appeal or reproach every line tells like a hammer-stroke.

Perdye I said it not,
   Nor never thought to do;
As well as I ye wott,
   I have no powre therto;
And if I ded, the lott,
   That first ded me enchain,
Do never slake the knott,
   But strayte it to my payne.

And if I ded, eche thing,
  That may do harm or woo,
Contynuallye maye wring
  My herte wherso I goo;
Reporte may alwayes ring
  Of shame of me for aye,
Yf yn my herte ded spring
  The worde that ye doo saye.

If I said so, eche sterre,
  That is in heven above,
May frowne on me to marre
  The hope I have yn love;
And if I ded, such warre,
  As they brought out of Troye,
Bring all my lyff afarre
  From all this lust and joye.

Nor does Wyatt at all foreshadow the Elizabethans, with their lavishness, their passion for visible things, their ready flow of coloured utterance. One phrase rings curiously with Sidney—

A hart I have besidis all this,
That hath my herte and I have his.

But Wyatt's real affinities, if with any, are with John Donne. He has not Donne's depth of fiery and often turbid thought. His is a soul of lighter make. But there is something of the same characteristic poise. Wyatt, too, can be a psychologist, watching his own emotions in detachment, with a finger on the burning pulse.

I must return from criticism to biography. The links between Wyatt's poetry and his recorded career are slight, and are to be found mainly in the sonnets and the *ottava rima* epigrams. A sonnet tells us that May was his unlucky month, and we know that May 1534 saw him in the Fleet, and May 1536 in the Tower. He writes an epigram to Sir Francis Bryan from prison; it might be either in 1536 or in 1541. Another sonnet begins—

> The piller pearishd is whearto I lent.

It is based on Petrarch's lament for his friend Giovanni Colonna, but it is not improbable that Wyatt adapted it to the fall of Cromwell. There are several references to his travels. A satire praises the cookery and deprecates the morals of France, Spain, Flanders and Rome. There are lines from Monçon in Spain, where he was in October 1537; others on a return from Tagus to the Thames; in others again he says,

> I follow the coles that be quent,
> From Dovor to Calais against my mynde.

An epigram, as it stands in Tottel, has the title *Of his loue called Anna*, and begins,

> What word is that, that changeth not,
>   Though it be turned and made in twaine:
> It is mine Anna god it wot.
>   The only causer of my paine.

In the Egerton MS. the third line has 'It is myn aunswer' but a second hand has added the title *Anna*, now half cut away from the paper. A balette in the Devonshire MS. is of 'That tyme that myrth dyd stere my shypp'. Wyatt recalls how,

> Then in my boke wrote my maystresse,
> 'I am yowris you may well be sure,
> And shall be whyle my lyff dothe dure'.

But now she is 'myn extreme enemye'. Later on in the manuscript, someone has written, among other scribblings in various hands upon a page which has no continuous poem,

> I ama yowrs
> An

A sonnet, again with a debt to Petrarch, tells of hunting a hind, but she eludes the poet,

> And graven with Diamonds in letters plain,
> There is written, her faier neck rounde abowte,
> Noli me tangere, for Cesars I ame.

Finally, there are lines upon a change of mistresses.

> By signe of love, then do I love agayne.
> If thou ask whome; sure, sins I did refrayne
> Brunet, that set my welth in such a rore,
> Thunfayned chere of Phillis hath the place
> That Brunet had; she hath and ever shal.

Here, too, there has been an alteration in the Egerton MS. The third line originally ran,

> Her that did set our country in a rore,

but Wyatt has altered it. We must, I suppose, being perhaps unreasonably curious about the private lives of poets, ask 'Who was Phillis, and who Brunet?' It certainly seems probable that Wyatt once had a love called Anna, and that, when he was preparing his poems for publication, he meant to expunge her from the record. There is not much to be made of the scribble in the Devonshire MS.; it might be merely by someone who had read the poem earlier in the book. That, however, does not give the apparent signature 'An'. Again, one might suppose the writer to be the A.I. or A.J., whose answer is appended to another of Wyatt's poems in the same manuscript. The tradition, however, in Wyatt's family was that he had been a lover of Anne Boleyn, and a story is told of a game of bowls, in which the King and Wyatt, in the presence of the Duke of Suffolk and Sir Francis Bryan, flaunted rival tokens from the lady, of which she was able to give the King a satisfactory explanation. Modern writers have generally pooh-poohed the tradition, but I am not sure that they are right. It is certain that, when Wyatt was sent to the Tower in 1536, contemporary observers believed him to be implicated in the charges against the queen. This is apparent both from the correspondence of the imperial ambassador with his court, and from that of John Hussey with Lord Lisle at Calais.[1] Hussey, at one time, thought that Wyatt would suffer with Anne's other paramours. No doubt gossip was misinformed; Henry and Cromwell were well enough able to keep their secrets. It is more likely that the chief object of Wyatt's arrest was to secure his evidence. No

[1] *L.P.* x, 353, 356, 380, 385, 386.

indictment seems to have been brought against him. Nor do letters of his father at this period show any great alarm.[1] On May 11 he writes to Cromwell, in return for a 'comfortable' message, hoping 'whensoever it shall be the king's pleasure with your help to deliver him, that ye will show him that this punishment that he hath for this matter is more for the displeasure that he hath done to God otherwise, wherein I beseech you to advertise him to fly vice and serve God better than he hath done'. And after the release he writes again of the King's 'great goodness' and 'favourable warnings' to his son, to whom he has himself 'not only commanded him his obedience in all points to the king's pleasure, but also the leaving of such slanderous fashion as hath engendered unto him both the displeasure of God and his master, and as I suppose I found it not now to do in him, but already done'. He writes also to the King in person, thanking him for not having chastised his son extremely. He is now himself old, and Thomas must supply his service, but if his truth were spotted, he would desire to see him perish before his face.

Wyatt's subsequent attitude towards his own imprisonment came up, as already noted, at his trial in 1541, and he asserted that he had always regarded it as due, not to Henry himself, but to the Duke of Suffolk. This has led ingenious minds to give a conjectural interpretation of some fragments of a conversation between Anne and Sir William

[1] *L.P.* x, 345, 349, 471; xi, 586.

Kingston, her keeper in the Tower, which, in spite of popular rumour, would dissociate his arrest altogether from her misdoings. The document is much torn, but these words are left.[1]

I also sayd Mr. Page and Wyet wase mo then she sayd he ha. . . one hys fyst tother day and ys here now bot ma. . . I shalle desyre you to bayre a letter from me. . . Secretory.

There is another reference at the end of the long conversation to Wyatt as a maker of 'balettes', but it throws no light on the earlier one. Sir Richard Page, a Gentleman of the Privy Chamber, was arrested with Wyatt, and also released. Dr Simonds thinks Anne may have said that Wyatt struck 'one with his fist the other day and is here now but many think he will soon be pardoned', and Professor Berdan elaborates this into a theory that the temper which had provoked a fray with the serjeants of London in 1534 had provoked another with men of the Duke of Suffolk in 1536.[2] I cannot feel that this is very plausible. A Tudor gentleman, ruffling it in the streets, would surely use a weapon other than his fist, and although a fray might lead to the Fleet, it would hardly lead to the Tower. Moreover, it is drastic to mend a tear in a paper by assuming the omission of a word from what remains un-mutilated. I will offer the counter-conjecture that what Anne said was that Wyatt had 'blown' or 'whistled' on his fist, meaning that he had played

[1] *L.P.* x, 338; H. Ellis, *Original Letters*, i, ii, 56.
[2] W. E. Simonds, *Sir Thomas Wyatt and his Poems* (1889), 33; Berdan, 464.

the informer. I cannot quote an exact parallel, but both the colloquial 'blow upon' and the Elizabethan 'whistle in the ear' have such a sense. And if so, the statement fits in with a story recorded by Nicholas Harpsfield in his *Treatise on the Pretended Divorce* as told to him by Antonio Bonvisi, a Luccan merchant long resident in London, who acted as banker for Henry's foreign loans.[1] According to this, Wyatt had been intimate with Anne before her marriage, and when he learnt that it was in prospect, told Henry of the fact, as a warning against her character. Henry commended his honesty and bade him keep the secret. Substantially the same account is in the *De Origine ac Progressu Schismatis Anglicani* of Nicholas Sanders.[2] Here the revelation is said to have been made in the first instance to the Privy Council, who put it before the King. Henry remained silent for a while, and then said that it was a lie. Wyatt, angry at his rebuff, told the Council that he could provide ocular demonstration of his relations with Anne. This was reported by the Duke of Suffolk to the King, but the suggestion offended Henry's sense of decency. He declared that Wyatt was an *audax et suspitiosus leno*, and added that he did not care for such *spectacula*. Wyatt was forbidden the court. The incident, says Sanders, proved his salvation, when Anne's misdemeanours ultimately came to light. Yet another version is to be found in the narrative known as the *Spanish Chronicle*, apparently

[1] Ed. N. Pocock (*Camden Soc.*), 253.    [2] Ed. 1585, 19.

a compilation made about 1550 by a Spanish
Catholic who, like Bonvisi, had been long in London, but who had only an outsider's knowledge of
political events.[1] He was an admirer of Wyatt, and
dwells on his popularity. 'This Master Wyatt was
a very gallant gentleman and there was no prettier
man at Court than he was'. He professes to give
a detailed account of an interview, after Anne's
arrest, between Wyatt and Cromwell, who had been
ordered by the King to examine him. 'The king
well knows', said Wyatt, 'what I told him before
he was married'. He went to the Tower, and thence
wrote a letter to the King, in which he reminded
him of the confession, and of his banishment from
court for two years as a result, and added a Boc-
caccio-like story of a trick which Anne once played
him at an assignation. The King sent for him.
'Wyatt, I am sorry I did not listen to thee when I
was angry, but I was blinded by that bad woman.'
There may be much embroidery here, and one
cannot give implicit credence to all that anti-
Protestant writers said about Henry's divorce and
its sequel. But in its main outline the story is
at least not inconsistent with what we know on
better authority about the facts of 1536. Sir Henry
Wyatt's letters certainly point to some moral offence
by the poet, rather than a mere fray. It is most
unlikely that he had anything to do with Anne
after her marriage. The King's intention to make
her his wife was still unknown to Wolsey in April

[1] Ed. M. A. S. Hume, 63, 68.

137

1527. A few months later it was common talk at court, and it is to this date that Wyatt's confession, if it took place, must be assigned. The detail that he was sent away from court for two years fits in with his absence on duty at Calais during 1528–30. Evidently the Duke of Suffolk had something to do with the affair. He was Henry's brother-in-law and in 1536 was Grand Master of the Household and a member of the special commission appointed to enquire into the treasons. It may very well have been he, rather than Henry, who directed Wyatt's arrest. And there is a bit of confirmatory evidence which has been overlooked. On May 10, 1530 Eustace Chapuys reported to the Emperor that Suffolk had long been absent from court.[1]

Et dit lon quil en est banny pour quelque temps a cause quil revela au Roy que la dame avoit este trouvee au delict avec ung gentilhomme de court, que desja en avoit autre-foys este chasse par suspicion, et ceste derriere foys lon lavoit aussy vuyde de la court a linstance de la dite dame qui fagnoit estre fort courrouce contre luy; mays enfin le Roy a intercede vers elle que le dite gentilhomme retournast a la court.

Wyatt is not named, but he has told us that a former mistress became his 'extreme enemye'. A descendant of the poet owned a small manuscript prayer-book, said to have been given to Anne's maid of honour, 'Mrs Wyatt', at her execution. We do not know that Margaret Wyatt was ever a maid of honour, and she was married to Sir Anthony Lee

[1] *Calendar of Spanish Papers*, IV (1), 535.

before Anne became queen. But she may very well have been one of the four ladies appointed to attend upon Anne in prison, and if so, the gift may not have implied any great affection, since with some of them she was not on good terms.[1] She may, therefore, have been hostile to Wyatt in 1530. And if Suffolk was then suspicious of Wyatt's good faith, his suspicions may very well have been renewed, and aggravated by a personal grievance, in 1536. On the whole, I think that the recorded facts and the contemporary gossip hang pretty well together.

Perhaps, then, we may after all re-establish the dark Anne Boleyn as the Brunet of Wyatt's lines. Certainly she set his country in a roar. Whether she was also the lady whom he followed as a quenched coal from Dover to Calais against his mind, we cannot tell. Many courtiers went with Henry and Anne, then Marchioness of Pembroke, for a meeting with Francis the First at Calais in 1532. We do not know that Wyatt was among them, but it is likely enough. Nor can we identify Phillis. Tottel's editor gives to the poem which begins ' Meruaile no more al tho' the title *The louers sorowfull state maketh him sing sorowfull songes, but Souche his loue may change the same*; and prints the last two stanzas as follows—

> But yet, perchance some chance
> May chance to change my tune:
> And when (Souch) chance doth chance
> Then, shall I thank fortune?

[1] *L.P.* x, 337.

And if I haue (Souch) chance:
Perchance ere it be long:
For (Souch) a pleasant chance,
To sing some pleasant song.

Here neither the Egerton nor the Devonshire MS.
nor *The Court of Venus* has the brackets or originally
read anything but 'such' or 'suche', but the word
has been omitted from the fifth line by the Egerton
scribe, and a later hand has supplied 'souche'.
There was in fact a Mrs Souche or Zowche in the
household of Queen Jane Seymour. Probably she
was Joan Rogers of Bryanston, Dorset, who married
Richard son of John Lord Zouch, and the 'M. Souch'
whose portrait by Holbein is at Windsor. But
'souche' is a recognised sixteenth-century spelling
of 'such', and it may be suspected that Grimald or
another was putting his own interpretation upon
Wyatt's rather fanciful phrasing. The romantic
Miss Foxwell suggests that Phillis was the Duchess
of Richmond, apparently for no other reason than
that she may have had something to do with the
Devonshire MS. I hope it was not so. The Duchess
was treacherous, like all the Howards, and helped
to swear her own brother's life away. Wyatt, a
poet, early separated from his wife, and living in an
age in which an irregular sexual relation was hardly
regarded as a slur upon a courtier's 'honesty', may
have had many amorous entanglements after 1527.
The contrast of Phillis with Brunet suggests that
she was a fair-haired lady. And of one such Wyatt
writes—

A face, that shuld content me wonders well,
  Shuld not be faire, but lovelie to behold,
With gladsome cheare all grief for to expell;
  With sober lookes so wold I that it should
Speake without wordes such wordes as non can tell;
  The tresse also shuld be of crysped gold.
    With witt and these might chaunce I might be tyde,
    And knyt agayne the knott that should not slide.

It so happens, however, that we can discover who
was the mistress of Wyatt's latest years. This is no
thanks to the *Dictionary of National Biography*,
which confuses the poet with his son. She was
Elizabeth Darrell, the daughter of Sir Edward
Darrell of Littlecote in Wilts, who had been vice-
chamberlain to Catharine of Aragon. Her sister
Jane married Sir Anthony Hungerford of Down
Ampney.[1] Elizabeth was one of Catharine's maids
on 14 March 1530, when an annuity of £10 was
granted her during the nonage of her nephew
Edward, the King's ward. With other ladies of the
queen's household, she refused to take the oath of
supremacy in 1534. Catharine left her a legacy of
£200 towards her marriage in 1536, and shortly
afterwards she approached Cromwell through Sir
Francis Bryan to secure payment of this, and to get
a post in the household of the new queen, since she
saw no hope in the Lady Mary.[2] Perhaps her
papistical leanings intervened, and she entered
instead the service of the Marchioness of Exeter,

[1] C. E. Long in *Wilts Archæological Magazine*, iv, 226;
H. Hall, *Society in the Elizabethan Age*, 185.
[2] *L.P.* v, 319; vii, 51; xi, 15, 358, 477.

whose father, Lord Mountjoy, had been Catharine's chamberlain. At any rate we find her in depositions of the autumn of 1538 which concern the conspiracy of the Marquis of Exeter and the Poles.[1] Lord Montague went to see her at Hackney about a debt due to her from Sir Anthony Hungerford, and told her of a plot to shoot Cardinal Pole in France. This she passed on to Sir Geoffrey Pole. Later she seems to have reported to Montague the escape of the Cardinal through the good offices of a French friend of Sir Francis Bryan. It is not quite clear which way her sympathies went. Nor does it much matter. What concerns us is the linking of her name and Wyatt's in the evidence of one Jerome Ragland, a servant of Montague, on October 28, 1538.

Last summer, being sent by Montacute to Elizabeth Darrell about assurance of certain lands, she said Mr. Wyatt was out of Spain, where he had been highly entertained, and that Mr. Wyatt said they had a poison in Spain, which put on an arrow head, and the same pricking any person, he should die, and the remedy was the juice of a quince or peach. She also said Mr. Wyatt saw Cardinal Pole 'but he spake not with him, nor one of them would not look on another'. Mr. Wyatt had told the King about the poison and asked if he should bring any hither, but the King answered 'Nay'.

This would have been in June 1538, when Wyatt broke his first Spanish embassy by a hasty visit to England, at the request of the Emperor, with a

[1] *L.P.* xiii (2), 268, 296, 300, 315, 334, 342, 343.

special communication for Henry. There is, of
course, nothing here to connect Wyatt with the
alleged plot to take the Cardinal's life. According
to Pole himself, a year later, Wyatt had boasted in
Spain that this would be done, in the event of his
being declared a public enemy to England.[1] Professor Merriman thinks that there is confirmation of
this in a despatch by Wyatt at the time of his recall,
which refers to something that he can only com-
municate to Henry by word of mouth.[2] But the
despatch itself is as cryptic. A fire may be kindled
in Italy, after the return thither of some unnamed
person. Possibly no more is meant than a scheme
to set jealousy between the Emperor and the King
of France about their rival claims to the possession
of Milan.[3] Doubtless, however, neither Henry nor
Wyatt would have been particularly scrupulous as
to the methods to be employed against a declared
public enemy. When Wyatt was sent to the Tower
for the second time in 1541, the King took possession of Allington Castle, and the directions from
the Privy Council to Sir Richard Southwell for
winding up the household there bade him 'enquire
of Mrs Darrell whether she intended to go to any
such place whereas she should be ordered, as that
wherwithal she appeared to be might be preserved;
and in case she would not declare to him the same,
whereby he might conjecture that might perish

---

[1] *L.P.* xiv (2), 63.
[2] *Life and Letters of Thomas Cromwell*, i, 211.
[3] *L.P* xiv (1), 216.

which she had conceived, then to stay her there, until the King's highness' further pleasure were known therein'.[1] Wyatt, by his will of 12 June, 1541, directed that lands should be settled on Elizabeth and her son Henry Darrell, *alias* Wyatt. This was done by the younger Sir Thomas, but the records name the son Francis.[2] Presumably Henry had died and this was a second son. The lands chosen were those of the dissolved priories of Tarrant Keynston in Dorset and Montacute in Somerset, which the poet had acquired by exchange with the crown. Elizabeth was living at Montacute in May 1546.[3] The payment of her annuity from the crown is traceable in the Chamber Accounts to the Christmas of 1548 and then stops.[4] The properties passed later to other families, in some cases at least under crown grants of 1554. It is to be inferred that Francis had also died without heirs, that the estate had reverted to the younger Sir Thomas under the remainder clause of the settlement, and had escheated to the crown on his treason in 1554.

Elizabeth Darrell, I suppose, whether she was Phillis or not, had her share in the poems. But it may be that, even in his own mind, Wyatt did not keep his chronicles quite distinct. His theme was love and the vicissitudes of love, rather than this or that woman. Enough, if from his garner of

[1] Nicolas, *P.C. Acts*, vii, 119.
[2] *L.P.* xvi, 229; xviii (1), 541; xix (1), 86; xxi (1), 78.
[3] *L.P. Addenda*, i (2), 583.
[4] *L.P. passim; Trevelyan Papers*, ii, 18.

experience he could draw something of absolute significance for expression in song. In the poetry of the emotions, as in the poetry of the supernatural, we are not to ask for literal transcripts. Here, too, we must only expect 'a semblance of truth sufficient to procure for these shadows of imagination that willing suspension of disbelief for the moment, which constitutes poetic faith'.

# The ENGLISH PASTORAL

THE Pastoral has fallen to a tarnished name, even among many who genuinely love their poets. It stands for something faded and fantastic; *hesterna rosa*, or rather, a rose which must even yesterday have been a scentless thing, a florist's flower. And yet this little instrument has discoursed most eloquent music; princes have breathed upon it in the palmy days of English song; ladies and scholars, a court and a people, have attuned their ears to the strains of its sweet piping. Now it lies broken and mute. King Pandion is dead;

> And Phillida the Fair has lost
> The comfort of her favour.

'A frigid pastoral'; in quite other sense than the 'cold pastoral' of Keats, the phrase has become a commonplace of ready criticism.

It is easy enough, in the light of literary history, to understand this ill repute of Arcadia. The eighteenth century made the pastoral ridiculous, and worse than ridiculous. Ridiculous, when Corydon, in ruffles and knee-breeches, piped it to a Phillis with patched cheeks and a ribbon on her crook; worse than ridiculous, when Marie Antoinette played the shepherdess in the gardens of Trianon, while the real peasants were dying upon their nettle-broth outside. Our great-grandfathers put away many conventions, both in life and art, with their full-bottomed wigs. Even of poetry they demanded a greater naturalism, a closer fidelity to the observed truth. When Crabbe was narrating the simple facts of the cottager's life, when Wordsworth was finding deep lessons of spiritual encouragement and consolation in the austere homes of Cumbrian dalesmen, there was no longer any room for the old conception of the singing shepherd. The 'swink'd hedger' ceased to be a mere element in the landscape; he became a human being, to be known and understood; a problem, not a plaything.

However, all this *was* in our great-grandfathers' days; and perhaps now, without injustice to the new spirit which they brought into literature, a spirit which has indeed recreated literature for us, we may be allowed to revise their somewhat impulsive condemnation. Indeed, whatever we may think of the eighteenth century—and it would be as wise to draw an indictment against a whole nation as against a whole century—it has not much to do with pastoral poetry. That had had its beginnings and its triumphs, its honourable career had ended in a peaceful grave, long before Pope plumed himself as the sole inheritor of the mantle of Spenser. The impudence, the ignorance of that boast! To annihilate the sweetest rhythms of Fletcher and Jonson and Milton; to blot out of the book of song, with one pedantic word, the names, the golden names, of Breton and Greene, of Drayton and Browne, of Herrick and Wither! One supposes that for Pope, steeped in his lore of Virgil and Theocritus, the pastoral meant only the formal eclogue. Untouched by the spirit of the thing, he never thought how the full stream of bucolic poetry had overleaped those narrow banks, to make vocal with its murmuring the lyric meads and the tangled woods of comedy.

Rightly to judge of the pastoral impulse in English verse we must look not to the eighteenth century, and not to the nineteenth, but strictly to the period between the coming of Elizabeth and that inauspicious moment, nearly a hundred years later, when Puritanism for a while snuffed out literature. Outside the drama, with only the fringes of which we are concerned, the poetry, and in a measure the prose, of that hundred years, is the outcome of two distinct and partly opposed waves of tendency. One does not like the expression, 'a school of poetry'; but it is difficult to dissociate the tendencies or tempers in question from the influence of two representative and dominant personalities, those of Spenser the musical, and of Donne the imaginative. On the one hand there is a body of poetry, transparent, sensuous, melodious, dealing with all the fresh and simple elements of life, fond of the picture and the story, rejoicing in love and youth, in the morning and the spring; on the other, a more complex note, a deeper thrill of passion, an affection for the sombre, the obscure, the intricate, alike in rhythm and in thought, a verse frequent with reflections on birth and death, and their philosophies, a humour often cynical or pessimistic, always making its appeal rather to the intellect than to the senses. The manner of Spenser and the manner of Donne, the Elizabethan style and the Jacobean, if you will; the two have to be carefully distinguished in any adequate treatment of the age. Yet either nomenclature is misleading; we have not to deal with two rival masters and two coteries of imitators, nor with two styles, whereof one at some moment of crisis or upheaval succeeded and replaced the other, as, for instance, the literature of the romantic revival succeeded and replaced the literature of the age of Pope. Rather we have to deal with two habits of thinking and writing, which belong to different and alternating tendencies in the one full life of a complex age, but which, throughout that age, co-existed and interpenetrated each other in a hundred ways. Certainly Spenser and Donne are the typical exponents of their respective groups; certainly the personal influence of either would be hard to overestimate; certainly the poetry of melody began earlier than the poetry of imagination; for in national as in individual life, the simple invariably comes before the complex, feeling precedes thought; but though the one temper grows and the other diminishes, still to the last they appear side by side, often directing in this mood and in that the harmonies of the same pen.

There can be no question that pastoral poetry is the proper province of those writers whom we have associated with the name of Spenser. Among them alone it reaches its complete and characteristic development. Donne and his fellows write pastorals, but the shepherd's smock sits awkwardly upon them. They twist the bucolic theme and imagery to the expression of alien emotions and alien ideas. The convention becomes too obvious. It is the philosopher in the hay-field; the hands are the hands of Esau, but the voice is the voice of Jacob. But to the Spenserian manner, with its simple attitudes and ideals, its simple delight in natural and spiritual beauty, the pastoral lends itself admirably. Even before Spenser wrote, a charming example had already appeared in Tottel's collection. In the interval Barclay and Googe had produced their stiff imitations of Virgil and Mantuan. But when *The Shepheardes Calender* was born, the breath of genius inspired the old forms with a Chaucerian freshness and a new melody. And from this moment the popularity of the pastoral was assured. It became the normal mode alike for panegyric and erotic verse. A shepherd stood as the well-understood symbol for a lover or a poet. A Spenser, a Sidney, had each his recognised poetic alias in Colin or Cuddie, Elphin or Philisides. Every branch of literature, lyric and sonnet, elegy and romance, comedy and mask, bears its marks of the pre-vailing fashion. The rich contents of the great miscellanies, above all, those of the *England's Helicon* of 1600, are but garlands woven from the finest blossoms of bucolic song.

It was Spenser, then, who first made the pastoral

a thing of significance for English writers; but he was by no means the creator of it as a literary species. We cannot claim here, as we can with a proper pride in the case of the contemporary romantic drama, to be dealing with an essentially national growth. The pastoral was an exotic, although an exotic which took kindly to English soil, and put forth fair flowers in English gardens. Moreover, it was an exotic which had been cultivated in Italy, and to a less degree in France, long before it reached our shores. The earliest vernacular Italian pastorals were written in the fifteenth century; by the beginning of the sixteenth they were already innumerable, and they continued in astonishing profusion for at least another hundred years.[1] In France the notable work of Clément Marot was produced between 1525 and 1544. It is not perhaps necessary to go very closely into the exact amount of the debt which our English bucolic writers owe to their continental predecessors. After all allowance has been made for the similarities which a recourse to common models would naturally bring about, it must still be very considerable. It is more to the purpose to point out that the whole of the pastoral literature of the Renaissance, whether in Italy, France, or England, was created out of elements gathered from the past, and to try to state briefly what those elements were.

[1] A large number are collected by G. Ferrario, in *Poesie Pastorali e Rusticali* (Classici Italiani, Milano, 1808). See also J. A. Symonds, *History of the Italian Renaissance*.

By far the most important was, of course, the *carmen bucolicum* or eclogue of classical antiquity. From the beginning, it would appear, the Aryan shepherds who dwelt in the pastoral districts of Greece shared in some humble measure the gift of song which became such a wonderful thing amongst their more highly favoured kinsmen of Attica. Even to-day the folk-song of those regions is full of delicate fancies and honeyed cadences which are unfamiliar to the peasantry of other lands.[1] The most complete development of this native popular poetry was reached by that branch of the nation which had migrated across the sea to the sunny shores of Sicily. There was the ideal country for the shepherd life; no chill turnip-fields or desolate downs, such as are our English pastures, but patches of rich meadow hollowed in the hills, with an outlook over the blue and laughing Mediterranean; cool caves overgrown with tangles of ten-drilled vine; soft beds of yellow cytisus and fragrant violet; clear springs bubbling up among tufts of myrtle and narcissus. There the cicala chirped at noonday, and the languid brown-limbed men and maidens kept watch over their little flocks of oxen or sheep or goats monotonously from dawn to eve. A land of immanent haunting deities; Artemis with the glimmer of white nakedness among the olives;

[1] See C. Fauriel, *Chants populaires de la Grèce moderne* (1825); Lucy Garnett, *Folk-song of Modern Greece*; and some remarks on the character of this poetry in the introduction to Mr Lang's translation of Theocritus.

Pan shaggy and jovial, all the lust and the trepidation of earth in his riotous gait; Daphnis, the very
indwelling spirit of the spring, the nympholept who
in the dog-days flung himself from a jutting head-
land to drown his sorrows in the cool wave beneath.
At the yearly festivals of these deities the shepherds
gathered themselves together to make merry, and
here the *carmen amoebæum*, the characteristic form
of Sicilian song, came into being. Rivalling each
other in alternate stanzas, the young men ex-
temporised chant after chant, now filled with rough
but good-humoured satire, now telling sweetly the
old legends of the country-side, or of rustic love-
making, or the simple incidents of the pastoral life.
Stesichorus of Himera, we are told, was the first,
some six centuries before Christ, to give literary
expression to this popular song. But the *Daphnis*
of Stesichorus is lost to us, and for practical purposes the creator of the pastoral as a deliberate
literary form is the Alexandrine Theocritus. Upon
Theocritus, a lover of the country, trapped in the
bustling decadent city and court life of Ptolemaic
Egypt, those bucolic rhythms, remembered so well
from his childhood, had all the fascination which
the simple exercises over the complex, a fascination
wrought out of contrast and reminiscence. He
wove them into poems of a delicate artificiality,
preserving the main outlines of the actual life from
which they sprang, but emphasising all the comely
elements therein, and rendering them with a
keener sense of natural beauty, a more subtle music

153

of the Doric speech, than ever yet glorified any oaten
pipe at any festival of Artemis. Certain traditional
forms Theocritus fixed upon the pastoral for all
time; the singing match for some rustic wager, a
soft white lamb, a carven drinking bowl of beech-
wood or of maple; the bout of rude bantering
between two rival swains; the sad lament of a lover for
unrequited or deceived love; the dirge of his fellows
around the tomb of some dead shepherd, Daphnis
or another, who in his time had himself well known
to build the lofty rhyme among them. These forms,
taken no doubt from actual memories of Himera or
Syracuse, Theocritus bequeathed to his successors in
the ways of the pastoral muse, and with them that
absorption in the amorous theme, which is after all
from beginning to end the dominant note of his lyric.

A band of disciples, less original than Theocritus
himself, crowded around him. Bion and Moschus,
each memorable for at least one poem of great
beauty, are the names left to us. Then, in the
triumph of Greek poetry over the austere Roman
conqueror, came Virgil, who translated the pastoral
of Theocritus to his own Italian fields, giving it
there a setting of vineyard and corn-land, brushing
off, it may be, some of the early freshness, but in its
place bestowing the polish of a yet more consum-
mate art. And so after Virgil, Calpurnius, and after
Calpurnius, Nemesianus,[1] and after Nemesianus

---

[1] H. Schenkl, *Calpurnii et Nemesiani Bucolica* (1885). The
eclogues of Calpurnius have been translated by Mr E. J. L. Scott
(1891).

the endless versifiers of the Christian centuries, each in his turn beating out the thin gold thinner, and producing, like the Platonic artist, his copy of a copy of a copy. With the Renaissance came new life to the Latin eclogue. It exactly hit the fancy of the humanists; they relished its artificial ring, the opportunities for covert satire upon Church and State which it afforded. Petrarch made use of it, and Boccaccio and Erasmus. Many of the essays of these neo-Latin writers, together with their classical and mediæval models, are to be found in a little volume published by Oporinus, at Basle, in 1546, under the quaint title of *En habes, lector, Bucolicorum auctores xxxviii.*[1] Of them all the most significant for the development of English litera-ture is the Carmelite, Baptista Spagnuoli Man-tuanus, the 'good old Mantuan' of *Love's Labour's Lost*, whose frigidly didactic eclogues impressed themselves on the imagination of Spenser and his contemporaries.

The main outlines of the classical eclogue are reproduced by the earlier writers of English pastoral with a fidelity which is often tedious. Of the modifications, in form and spirit, to which it gradually lent itself, we must speak directly: but we have first to note that, in all bucolic poetry and

[1] The full title runs *En habes, lector, Bucolicorum auctores xxxviii quotquot a Virgilii aetate ad nostra usque tempora eo poematis genere usos, sedulo inquirentes nancisci in praesentia licuit, Farrago quidem eclogarum clvi mira cum elegantia tum varietate referta.*

prose as it was cultivated at the Renaissance, we find united with the eclogue elements of less importance from other strata of literary tradition, tributaries which mingled half imperceptibly with the waters of the main stream. For, after all, the shepherd life is a familiar thing all the world over, nor could it be expected that at one point or in one manner only it should leave its mark upon human thought and human art. Three of these secondary influences helped to form the sixteenth-century pastoral. Firstly, there is the remarkable novel, *Daphnis and Chloe*, in which, about the fifth century after Christ, the Greek prose-writer Longus strove to give an entirely new form to the conventions of Theocritus.[1] *Daphnis and Chloe*, with its early traces of 'romantic' love, its early passion for scenery, is undeniably a notable ancestor of the later pastoral developments of the romance, as they present themselves in Sannazaro, in Montemayor, in Sidney. Secondly, there is the *pastourelle* of mediæval France, a short lively poem—half dialogue, half recital—in some degree Provençal in its origin, and always constant to a single type of structure. A noble youth meets a shepherdess in the fields; he dismounts to woo her, is successful or unsuccessful in his love, and in either event mounts and rides away. The *pastourelles* of the troubadour Colin Musset are lost to us, but in the thirteenth century

[1] *Daphnis and Chloe* was translated into English, from the French of Amyot (1559), by Angel Day in 1587, and this translation has been reprinted by Mr Joseph Jacobs (1890).

the form was dramatised by Adam de la Halle in his *Jeu de Robin et Marion*, which still exists.[1] The typical incident of the *pastourelle* has left its trace upon the love-stories of Florizel, and of many another disguised Elizabethan prince; and the name of Robin recurs in the eclogues of Clément Marot, to which the author of *The Shepheardes Calender* recognises his debt. And finally, one must not leave out of account the pastoral affinities in the one book which of all others most profoundly impressed the Englishmen of the sixteenth century. The Old and the New Testament, accessible at last in the splendid new words of Tyndale and of Coverdale, yielded each its episodes of pastoral life. The Old gave them David, with his idyllic boyhood among the sheep-folds; the New that wakeful night of the shepherds under the same starry heavens of Bethlehem, already a theme familiar for its quaint renderings in the miracle-plays of the north; nor could it be forgotten how in parable deliberate choice had been made of the Good Shepherd to serve as symbol for the Founder of Christianity himself, of the faithful shepherd and the hireling as types respectively of the just and the unjust amongst his appointed teachers. So that 'pastoral' came to have its clear ecclesiastical signification, and it fell out naturally for Spenser or Milton to adapt to the bucolic forms their allegories of the religious life. And it was characteristic of the medley of ideas which everywhere distinguishes

[1] Bartsch, *Altfranzösische Romanzen und Pastourellen* (1870).

Renaissance art, that the pastoral should thus absorb
into itself pagan and religious elements, and present
them side by side without fear of incongruity;
Peter mourning in the company of Triton and the
Muses over the hearse of Lycidas, while 'the mighty
Pan' must do duty in *The Shepheardes Calender*,
alike for the wood-god of classical myth, for the
historic Henry the Eighth, and for the very person
of the Almighty.

The Latin writers of pastoral adhered precisely
to the manner of the formal eclogue.[1] The varieties
of this fell within comparatively narrow limits.
Sometimes descriptive, it was more often dramatic
or pseudo-dramatic in its setting, the dialogue or
monologue, generally interspersed with songs, of
imagined shepherds. The metre was invariably the
hexameter; the typical situations followed the
models already set by Theocritus and Virgil. The
eclogue, thus constituted, by no means disappeared

---

[1] *Eclogues*, ἐκλογαί, are literally 'selections'. The name is given
in MSS. to the bucolics of Virgil, Calpurnius, and Nemesianus,
and to certain short astronomical poems of Ausonius. The Elizabethans misunderstood and mis-spelt the word. Thus, in the
Generall Argument to *The Shepheardes Calender*, E. K. writes
'*Æglogai*, as it were αἴγον, or αἰγονόμων λόγοι, that is,
Goteheards tales'.

*Idyll*, εἰδύλλιον, is the name for a short descriptive poem, and
means literally 'a little picture'. The name was applied both to the
pastoral and the mythological poems of Theocritus. The Romans
of the Empire used both 'eclogue' and 'idyll' as general names for
a short poem. Cf. Pliny, *Epistles*, IV, 14, 9, 'sive epigrammata sive
idyllia sive eclogas...sive poematia vocare malueris'.

*Bucolic* is derived from the Greek βουκόλος, a herdsman.

at the Renaissance. Spenser and Drayton, to name
no others, were content to accept its broad outlines. But even they reject the classical uniformity
of metre. Googe, indeed, confines himself to mono-
tonous seven-foot lines[1]; but Spenser uses a be-
wildering variety of rhythms, and makes a further
distinction, within each eclogue, between the metre
of the dialogue and that of the more lyrical portions.
Even these innovations left the formal eclogue stiff
and constrained in its English dress. The path of
development for the Elizabethan pastoral lay in
the direction of still enlarged liberty. Those who
handled it most successfully, while maintaining the
essential features of the old bucolic convention, the
scenery, the *dramatis personæ*, the traditional range
of sentiment and emotion, yet allowed themselves
extreme freedom of choice as to the forms in which
they gave it expression. Thus it was that the pastoral
came to invade almost every sphere of literature,
and notably those of drama and romance.

Pastoral drama may be said to begin, in Italy,
with the *Favolo di Orfeo* of Politian in 1472. Its
two masterpieces were the *Aminta* of Torquato
Tasso (1573), and the *Pastor Fido* of Guarini
(1590); delicately sensuous love-poems these, full
of colour and sunshine and song, already containing
in the abundance of their lyrical elements the germs
of the Italian opera that was to be. In England, the
pastoral drama found itself a home at court, where

[1] Barnabe Googe, *Eglogs, Epytaphes, and Sonettes* (1563),
edited by Prof. Arber in his *English Reprints* (1871).

159

everything artificial was sure of a welcome from Elizabeth. Sir Philip Sidney's masque, *The Lady of the May*, was presented before her at Wanstead in 1578, and was followed, a few years later, by Peele's pretty comedy, *The Arraignment of Paris* (1581?), in which the scene is set among the flocks of Ida. The sub-plot tells of the loves of Colin and Thestylis, while in the main action, by a flattery not too gross to hit its mark, the golden apple which moved such divine discord is bestowed in a full council of heaven upon the Virgin Queen. In the comedies written by Lyly for boy actors from 1584 to 1590, as in the 'entertainments' of this, and the court masks of the next reign, pastoral elements repeatedly occur. Shakespeare glorified the prevailing fashion in *As You Like It* (1599–1600), and in the fourth act of *A Winter's Tale* (1610–11). Fletcher modelled upon the *Pastor Fido* his own *Faithful Shepherdess* (1608–09), and Jonson interwove a shepherd story with the legends of Robin Hood in his memorable fragment of *The Sad Shepherd* (before 1637). Works of less genius are Rutter's *Shepherd's Holiday* (1635), Goffe's *Careless Shepherdess* (publ. 1636, acted before 1629), and Randolph's *Amyntas* (1638); while Day in his *Isle of Gulls* (1606), and Shirley in his *Arcadia* (publ. 1639, acted 1632?), adapted to the purposes of the stage certain episodes from Sidney's famous romance.

For pastoral fiction, as well as pastoral comedy, looked to Sidney as its English Hippocrene. His

*Arcadia* was the third of the three great sixteenth-century romances. The Italian *Arcadia* of Giacomo Sannazaro had preceded it in 1504, and the Spanish *Diana Enamorada* of the Portuguese Jorge di Montemayor in 1542. In these interminable tales the pastoral novel of Longus is wedded to the dying mediæval romance. At one moment the hero is performing wonders of chivalry, at another he is disguised as a shepherd, making love to a shepherdess, herself in truth only a disguised princess. The *Arcadia* was begun at Wilton in 1580, for the amusement of the author's sister, Mary, Lady Pembroke. Sidney was then under a cloud at court, and must have gladly sought the solace of meadow and garden, and the congenial tasks of literature. The *Arcadia* was not intended for the world, and Sidney requested on his death-bed that it might be destroyed. Lady Pembroke, however, decided otherwise, and it appeared, pieced together from the scattered sheets on which it was written, in 1590. Like its foreign predecessors, it is a medley of prose and verse, verse which in Sidney's case, at least, is often neither relevant to the story, nor in itself delightful, being for the most part indiscreet exercises in the 'English versifying', the exotic metres, which it was at one time the creed of Sidney and his group to impose upon English song. For detailed analysis or criticism of the *Arcadia* I have no space here. Tedious it is, yet full of beauty, and instinct with a high seriousness, by no means meriting its author's contemptuous dismissal as 'vain, vain, vain', or Milton's echoed denunciation of a 'vain, amatorious poem'. It set a fashion, although it had no successors of importance; the new affectations of the style replaced the earlier euphuism of Lyly; the matter did much to extend the popularity of pastoralism. It is probably to Sannazaro and to Sidney that we owe the substitution of Arcadia for Sicily as the traditional home of the pastoral life, though here they do but expand a hint in the seventh eclogue of Virgil, where Corydon and Thyrsis are spoken of as '*Arcades ambo*'.

Sidney was not the only man to adapt the pastoral to the purposes of prose fiction. Between the time of the writing and the publication of the *Arcadia*, Greene, Lodge, and others had already begun to occupy the field with short pamphlet novels, conceived in a pastoral vein. These were based rather on the Italian *novelle* than on the heroic romance. The two best of them, Lodge's *Rosalynde* (1590), and Greene's *Dorastus and Fawnia* (1588), are well worth reading, apart from the fact that they served as material to be transmuted by the incomparable art of Shakespeare. Nor is the influence of the pastoral to be found only in the drama and the romance. It meets us in the love-sonnet, in the epic, in the allegorical poem. Lodge indites his *Phillis Honoured with Pastoral Sonnets* (1593); Spenser introduces Pastorella and her 'lustie shepheard swains' into the sixth book of *The Faerie Queene*; Phineas Fletcher puts the tedious disquisitions of *The Purple Island* into the mouth of the shepherd Thirsil. Through this breaking down of literary barriers, the shepherds often find themselves in strange company. With the gods and goddesses, the nymphs and satyrs, of pagan mythology, they may be thought not incongruous, although in Theocritus these have no part, save as objects of legend and worship. But they are distinctly less at home with the spirits of another sort, the elves and fairies of Celtic and Teutonic folk-lore, with whom they are sometimes, as in Drayton's *Muses' Elizium*, called upon to appear.

We have spoken of the eclogue proper, of the pastoral drama and the pastoral romance, of the overflow of pastoral into other fields of literature, and yet we have left untouched the chief glory of Elizabethan pastoral. This is assuredly the pastoral lyric. From the time of Theocritus the introduction of songs had been a regular feature of eclogue. These had often but a very slight connection in subject with the dialogue in which they were inserted. Spenser had further given them a metrical independence. It was but a short step to detach them entirely from their setting, to treat them as self-contained lyrical poems. From such lyrics the poetic anthologies of the day, *England's Helicon* and the rest, derive much of their peculiar charm; they star the pages of innumerable song-books. But whether isolated or included in eclogue, drama, and romance, there is nothing in the whole of Elizabethan literature more purely felicitous than the

163

pastoral songs and short descriptive pieces of simple rhythm, which poured in such profusion from the pens of Lodge and Greene, of Breton and Campion, and many another less famous writer. They bubble over with woodland music, the notes of the birds in spring, the rhythms of falling waters. Nor at a later period are Herrick and Marvell, this in his sober, that in his pagan mood, less happy in the same kind of composition. Many might hold that it is in the *Corinna's Going A-Maying*, or in *The Mower to the Glowworms* that English bucolic poetry reaches its high-water mark.

These, then, are the main forms in which Elizabethan pastoral shaped itself. We turn to another aspect of the matter. The genius which creates a novel mode of literature or art must necessarily leave a heritage of difficulty for those who come after. It is so hard at all times to steer clear of the exact point where discipleship ends and imitation begins. Just as the domineering individuality of Pope—

> Made poetry a mere mechanic art,
> And every warbler has his tune by heart,

so, in the region of pastoral, the fascinating individuality of Theocritus became a standing danger in the path of his successors. Theocritus sang of themes that he knew well, of the scenery and the society familiar to his boyhood. His idylls were a poet's transcript from actuality. So haunting were his memories, so vivid his pictures, that their

164

influence hung like an atmosphere over all subsequent attempts of other men to render the pastoral life in song. His incidents, his very phrases, became a common stock upon which all who followed him drew alike. But the difference between model and copy is a fundamental one. When Theocritus' descriptions of Sicilian shepherds were transferred to other lands, they naturally lost all such realistic elements as they possessed, and took on the character of mere convention. The habitual daily life of the slopes of Etna could only be fantasy in the meadows of Kent, or even upon the plain of Lombardy. Probably the shepherds of Mantua never sang against each other for a cup of white maple wood, whereon was wrought the loves of Ares and Aphrodite, with a border of acanthus leaves; certainly this was not the form of competition celebrated at the meeting at which Master Page's fallow greyhound was 'outrun on Cotsall'.

Thus, as is the case with all art that depends mainly upon reproduction, the pastoral was in a constant state of menace from the artificial elements in it; the liberal use of conventions threatened conventionality; the poetry was always on the point of degenerating into a mere literary exercise. Nor can it be denied that, for long periods together, this fate actually did overtake it; after Virgil, for instance, and after, or perhaps, not only after, Pope. And part of the interest of the history of pastoral, during its more vigorous and productive seasons, is in the study of the various methods

165

by which different writers strove to overcome this tendency, to revitalise a decadent tradition. Four ways in which this process of revitalising has been attempted may be profitably distinguished. The first two have this in common, that they introduce elements quite alien to the pastoral life, treating of that, not for its own sake, but only as a symbol of what actually occupies the mind of the writer. There is the method of personal allusion. The poet brings in himself, his friends, his mistress, in the guise of shepherds and shepherdesses, and under that transparent veil, indulges in what is always so attractive, both to author and to readers, autobiography. Such a course offers many delights. It has its flavour of enigma, the perpetual interest of a partly revealed mystery. It affords abundant opportunities for the compliment discreetly insinuated, for the attack which gathers sting from its indirectness, above all, for the love poem which may dare to be warm without audacity, inasmuch as the very artificiality of the form really permits the closer approach. To Rosalind or Idea you may safely sing what Rose Dyneley or Anne Goodyere might think fit to deem impertinent. The personal note can hardly be traced now, if it ever existed, in Theocritus; but the dead shepherd of Moschus' lament is clearly his fellow-poet Bion, and in Virgil the fortunes of the poet himself are put in the mouth of Tityrus, while the adventures of his noble friends, Pollio and Gallus, are his frequent theme. The eclogues of Calpurnius are devoted to the laudation of Nero;

in Petrarch, Pamphilus and Mition stand for St Peter and Clement the Sixth; while Boccaccio introduces the Emperor and the City of Florence under the pastoral names of Daphnis and Florida. The recurrence of the same device in English pastoral is too obvious to need proof. The extent to which it was carried may best be seen in Spenser's *Colin Clout's Come Home Again.* Here we have Spenser himself figuring as Colin, Gabriel Harvey as Hobbinol, Raleigh as the Shepherd of the Ocean. Moreover, a large part of the poem is occupied by an account of all the poets and the great lords and ladies whom Spenser met in London, each duly labelled with a pastoral appellative. Elizabeth heads the list as Cynthia, and the rest follow, to the number of twenty or thirty; nor can we doubt that, although many of the names are difficult for us to identify, they were all well understood by, at any rate, the inner literary circles of the day.

But from personal allusion it is only a short step to political, social, or religious allusion. At one time pastoral became allegorical, or, at the least, didactic. This phase of development belongs mainly to the beginning of the Renaissance. The *Pollio* of Virgil is not strictly a pastoral at all. The poet admittedly leaves the humbler theme to launch into his prophecy of national greatness—

Sicelides Musae, paullo maiora canamus.

The humanists, however, were not slow to recognise in the pastoral a powerful weapon for the

purposes of satire. A large number of the eclogues
contained in the volume published by Oporinus
are in reality but thinly veiled attacks upon Church
and State, Papacy and Empire. Mantuan, again,
is mainly concerned to moralise; a fact which
doubtless explains the unexampled popularity of
his work as a text-book for grammar-schools. And
here comes in that easy parallel, already alluded to,
between the shepherd, the *pastor*, and the priest
or clergyman. Piers and Palinode, the disputing
shepherds in the fifth eclogue of the *Shepheardes
Calender*, stand for the Protestant and the Catholic
divine; and in the seventh and ninth eclogues the
theme is repeated. Perhaps it speaks well for the
literary sense of the Elizabethans that this particular mode of treating pastoral proved, on the whole,
a trifle too tedious for them, and practically
vanished out of account. Its influence, however,
may be easily traced in the passage about 'the
hungry sheep' in Milton's *Lycidas*.

It is obvious that poetry which appeals to its own
time, not through inherent literary qualities, but by
force of personal or social allusion, must lose pro-
portionately in its hold upon posterity. The two
remaining methods by which the failing energies of
pastoral have been from time to time refreshed and
recreated, are not open to the same objection. They
rest upon broad permanent tendencies of human
nature, the twin faculties of imagination and
observation, the instincts, if you will, towards
realism and idealism. And these two lines of

development are by no means incompatible; in
the finest Elizabethan pastoral they proceed, in
large measure, side by side. It was possible, while
preserving the main outlines of the pastoral convention, to bring it subtly into touch with English
life; substituting the scenery, the manners and
customs, the legends and superstitions of our own
country-side for those which so many since Theocritus had borrowed from Sicily; letting the hawthorn bloom instead of the cytisus, and the dog-rose
take the place of the trailing vine. Such a process,
carried too far, would end in destroying the pastoral altogether; it would lead to a new poetry of
nature and rural life, such as later ages have
given us. And good as this is, it is good in another
way from pastoral, whose highest function, as we
shall see directly, is to paint an imaginary and not
a real life. But perhaps the fault of the Elizabethans
is, that they did not carry the process quite far
enough. In fact, the ways of the country were a
little beyond their sphere of observation. Touches
of landscape, of hill and meadow, of copse and
river, they give us in plenty; but the life of the
peasant, as it was lived in the plains of Warwickshire or on the Wiltshire downs, was a sealed book
to all but the greatest of them. Even Spenser,
wearing some part of the mantle of his father,
Chaucer, is not always happy in his attempts to be
natural; his cumbrous English names, his fantastic
Northumbrian dialect, are only clumsy instead of
being rustic. Here and there, in Spenser himself, in

his humbler follower Basse, in the wayward Herrick,
some genuine knowledge of farm and sheepfold
and village green mingles with the verse; but such
impulses were always isolated, and without much
effect upon the main body of pastoral literature.

On the other hand, the imaginative or idealist
way of treating the pastoral appealed very strongly
to the Elizabethan temper. Consider for a moment
some of the social conditions of the age. City life,
as we now know it, was just beginning to make
itself felt as an element in English society. Literature was coming more and more to centre in London, and London was already growing oppressive.
Certainly, from any part of it, you could still reach
the fields in a ten-minutes' walk; the frog-bit, as
Gerarde tells us, was yet to be found in the pools
and ditches of Southwark. Nevertheless, the life
of the day was essentially one lived among men,
and not among trees. And further, the old order
of things, in which each found from birth some
natural place and definite sphere of duties marked
out for him, had disappeared; the struggle for
existence, though the term would not have been
understood, was becoming exacting; a man must
push and bustle and intrigue and trample upon his
fellows, to make his own way. Life was strenuous
and difficult, and though it had its ardours and
extreme joys, it had its moments of weariness and
reaction also. The finer spirits of the day were
clearly touched to this issue; Ralegh yearning for
his 'scallop shell of quiet'; Spenser going home

with a sigh of relief to the 'green alders by the
Mulla's shore', or Donne to the 'salads and onions
of Mitcham'. And it was to this mood that pastoral
had its pleasant meaning. For one must realise
that pastoral is not the poetry of country life, but
the poetry of the townsman's dream of country
life. Upon the semblance of such a dream is
Arcadia fashioned; a land of rustling leaves and
cool waters, of simple pleasures and honest loves;
a land where men 'fleet the time carelessly, as they
did in the golden world', untroubled so long as
their flocks bear well, and their mistresses are kind,
content with rude lodging and humble fare, and
without envy for the luxuries and vexations of the
great. Three spiritual notes characterise the pastoral. One is this exaltation of content, connecting
itself on the one side with the longing for renewed
simplicity of manners, on the other with a vivid
sense of the uncertainty of all human advantages.
In this key you have Greene, with his—

> Ah, what is love? it is a pretty thing,
> As sweet unto a shepherd as a king;
> And sweeter too;

or Dekker, with his—

> Art thou poor, yet hast thou golden slumbers?
> O, sweet content!
> Art thou rich, yet is thy mind perplexed?
> O, punishment!

In that, the solemn dirges of Shakespeare—

> Golden lads and girls all must,
> As chimney-sweepers, come to dust;

and of Shirley—

> The glories of our blood and state
> Are shadows, not substantial things;
> There is no armour against fate;
> Death lays his icy hand on kings:
> Sceptre and crown
> Must tumble down,
> And in the dust be equal made
> With the poor crooked scythe and spade.

Then there is the note of love; the one serious preoccupation of the pastoral life, running like a golden thread through the whole of its literature. And here again it is a love mainly enamoured of simplicity; as of the courtier, wearied out by maids of honour, with their airs and graces, and finding an exquisite pleasure in the shy words and open heart of Phyllida or Amaryllis.

And finally, there is the note of delight in, and refreshment from, natural beauty. Our poems are full of spring and of the voice of birds, diapered with flowers of every hue and savour, whether it be the familiar flowers of hedgerow and meadow, the daffodils and cowslips making a cloth of gold, the tangles of eglantine and woodbine, or the homely denizens of the cottage garden, pansies and columbines and marigolds, larkspurs and lilies—

> lilies of all kinds,
> The flower-de-luce being one.

It is nature, indeed, as it presented itself to the Elizabethans, somewhat vaguely and generally conceived. There is none of that accurate observation which Darwin has taught our modern poets, any more than there is that haunting sense of immanent deity which they have inherited from Wordsworth. The times and seasons of a country calendar are rarely observed, the habits of fauna and flora imperfectly understood. 'Milton's lark', says Mr Arthur Sidgwick, 'which came in spite of sorrow to bid good morrow at his window (in the village of Horton) was certainly a redbreast. Lycidas' laureate hearse is to be strewn with three kinds of berries and eleven kinds of flowers; but the unfortunate Edward King was drowned on the 10th of August, when none of the berries would have appeared, and nine of the eleven flowers would be over.'[1] Spenser mingles damask roses with the daffodillies and primroses of Elisa's 'cremosin coronet', and bids the maidens bring both 'coronations' and king-cups for her adorning. Only Shakespeare is careful to make Perdita distribute the proper flowers of middle summer from her nosegay, and lament the absence of the flowers of spring that might furnish fitting garlands for her girl friends. These are perhaps the incidents of rural poetry as the townsman writes it; yet one is inclined to think that they point to a deeper divergence of the Elizabethan point of view from our own. Nature for them was a thing only to be felt, not studied; emotion was its interpreter and not science. They caught the fresh innocent delight of childhood, and were content to miss the subtler, if

[1] *Poets and Insects*, in *The Pelican Record* for June, 1893.

ιot higher, pleasures which come of greater knowledge and understanding.

Shakespeare, in the plenitude of his insight, has
left us what we may take as a criticism of the
philosophy of life which underlies the pastoral.
In *As You Like It* he paints the ideal with a full
sense of its beauty, yet not without his touches of
irony also. 'Sweet are the uses of adversity' is the
motto of the outlaws; but this is not quite the final
conclusion which the working out of the play
illustrates. Jaques, the disillusioned libertine, and
Phebe, the disdainful shepherdess, are discordant
elements in the forest. Minds innocent and quiet,
Rosalind or Orlando, or the Duke, may take it for
an hermitage; but it has no amulet to heal the dis-
contented and the froward. With this judgement of
the wise master we may leave the matter.

There is, however, one farther and in some
measure isolated aspect of the pastoral spirit which
calls for remark. The 'pastoral melancholy' is by
no means part of the ideal which we have been
considering. There the shepherd life is uniformly
considered as blithe and joyous, unvexed by any
sorrow that time or song cannot readily cure. But
in reality, the life of the fields is never without its
undertone of sadness. Clear away the fripperies of
civilisation, put yourself into touch with the great
heart of things, and the primal tragedies of existence, the burden of labour and the pang of loss,
become, not less, but more affecting. In the hush
of the woods and pastures, the 'still sad music of

humanity' is plainly audible. And if you go back to Theocritus, only another way of returning from convention to reality, the echo of this music rarely ceases to sound. Especially did such sentiment tend to connect itself with the idea, always so intolerable to the pagan imagination, of death. We have already noted, among the primitive modes of Sicilian song, the dirge for some dead comrade, or in commemoration of the mythical herdsman, Daphnis. Bion has left us a literary adaptation of such a theme. And when Bion himself died, Moschus used the form to express, in poetic metaphor, the sorrow of those who had loved him for the lost singer and friend. In our own literature it has become traditional for such a purpose. Again and again throughout the centuries

> The same sweet cry no circling seas can drown
> In melancholy cadence rose to swell
> Some dirge of Lycidas or Astrophel,
> When lovely souls and pure, before their time,
> Into the dusk went down.[1]

Philip Sidney and Edward King, John Keats and Arthur Clough, all alike cut off by an ineluctable fate in the flower of their days; for all alike the cadences of a half-forgotten Greek poet have woven their imperishable memorial.

The interest of the history of English pastoral ends abruptly with the seventeenth century. With

[1] J. W. Mackail, *On the Death of Arnold Toynbee*, in *Love's Looking-Glass* (1891).

the rise of Pope we pass from the age of literature to the age of literary intrigue. Pope's four pastorals were written, according to his own statement, at the age of sixteen. It is probable that he somewhat exaggerated his own precocity. They were published in Tonson's *Miscellany* in 1709, at the end of a volume which opened with another set of pastorals by Ambrose Philips. Some years afterwards a series of critical papers upon pastoral poetry appeared in Steele's periodical, the *Guardian*,[1] in which Philips' work was singled out for the very highest praise. The writer, who is conjectured to have been Tickell, spoke of 'Theocritus, who left his dominions to Virgil; Virgil, who left his to his son Spenser; and Spenser, who was succeeded by his eldest born Philips'. Pope was bitterly offended at this preference of his rival, and contrived a characteristic revenge. He wrote an essay in which his own pastorals were compared with those of Philips, and which was designed to display the real superiority of the former, while giving an ironical advantage to the latter. This he sent anonymously to Steele for the *Guardian*. Steele, good honest man, failed to see the intended irony, and thought it desirable to obtain Pope's leave before publishing the paper. This Pope was generously pleased to grant. It must be admitted that Steele's mistake is perfectly intelligible. Not only had Pope, after the manner of Defoe in his *Shortest Way with Dissenters*, so overdone the irony as to obscure the point, but

[1] *Guardian*, Nos. 22, 23, 28, 30, 32.

also the poetic superiority, which he intended the passages quoted from his own pastorals to show over those taken from Philips, is by no means as manifest as he thought. However, the paper duly appeared in the *Guardian* for April 27, 1713,[1] and Philips at least was at no loss as to the purport of it. His reply was effective, although it passed the limits of literary warfare. He hung up a birch in the coffee-room at Button's, and threatened to use it upon his 'rival Arcadian' if he dared to set foot in that popular resort.

Certainly, the controversy as to the respective merits of Pope and Philips has lost its freshness. From the point of view taken in this essay, each had failed alike to appreciate the true conditions and to catch the proper spirit of pastoral. Yet within their own limits, one can hardly deny that the superiority rests with Pope. The contrary judgement were to confuse a rhymester with a man of genius. Pope's manner is intolerably artificial; he bears the graceless yoke of the Miltonic epithet; his matter is a mere pastiche from Virgil and Theocritus, Dryden and Spenser; but for melodious rhythm and dignity of phrase his pastorals reach a point which he never afterwards surpassed. The musical possibilities of the heroic couplet are exhausted in the eclogue entitled *Autumn*, and though we may perhaps think the metre inappropriate to the subject, we cannot fail to be sensible of the ease and dignity of the verse.

[1] *Guardian*, No. 40.

Eighteenth-century criticism occupied itself a good deal with the laws and nature of bucolic poetry. Pope, Addison, and Johnson contributed something to the discussion of the theme;[1] but they all proceeded upon the impossible lines laid down by the French critic and poet Fontenelle in his *Discours sur la Pastorale*.[2] Fontenelle's idea was to establish principles which should guide the poet in his representation of rustic life. Theocritus was too realistic, Virgil too remote from the subjects of which he treated. The proper method was to strike a middle course between the opposed dangers of barbarity and over-refinement. A very characteristic eighteenth-century doctrine, but not one calculated to afford poetical inspiration. It was the gravamen of Pope's criticism of Philips that he was too rude, that he departed from the dignity of pastoral by an attempt to paint English instead of Sicilian country life, and by introducing such English names as Hobbinol and Lobbin for the time-honoured Alexis and Thyrsis. Herein of course Philips was only following the model already set by Spenser. Pope was not content with the practical joke played in the *Guardian*, and devised a new means of throwing ridicule upon his enemy. He proposed to Gay to write some burlesque

[1] Pope in his *Guardian* paper, and in his *Essay* prefixed to his *Pastorals*; Addison in the *Spectator*, No. 523; Johnson in the *Rambler*, Nos. 36, 37, and the *Adventurer*, No. 92.
[2] Bernard Le Bovier de Fontenelle, *Poésies Pastorales avec un traité sur la Nature de l'Eglogue* (1698).

pastorals which should parody Philips by carrying rusticality to an extravagant pitch. Gay took the hint, and in 1714 appeared *The Shepherd's Week*. The satirical design is evident enough in the affected use of obsolete words, in the absurd bumpkin nomenclature, Buxoma and Blouzelind, Clumsilis and Hobnelia. But Gay's poetic instinct was too much for him. He had a true insight into the picturesque elements of rural life, a wide knowledge of country customs and country superstitions. And so, though only half intending it, he produced no mere parody, but a genuine work of pastoral art, the nearest approach to a realistic pastoral which our literature had yet seen. And here the history of pastoral really closes upon a note curiously significant. The versifiers who followed in the wake of Pope are of no account. But the temper of Gay, so fantastic in his own age, is prophetic enough to us of the tendencies, revolutionary and deep-rooted, which were destined, nearly a century later, to transform completely the English conception of country life as a subject for poetry. Our modern literature is intimate with the woods and fields, conversant with the dwellers therein. You might gather a philosophy and a natural history of the peasant from George Eliot and Thomas Hardy alone. But the ideals of the past are illusions in the eyes of the present; and, save as a rare survival or a conscious archaism, the fine old art of pastoral has given way to newer and more vital modes of thought and imagination. Let

the authoress of *A Village Tragedy* write its
epitaph—

> Peace, Shepherd, peace! What boots it singing on?
> Since long ago grace-giving Phœbus died,
> And all the train that loved the stream-bright side
> Of the poetic mount with him are gone
> Beyond the shores of Styx and Acheron,
> In unexplorèd realms of night to hide.
> The clouds that strew their shadows far and wide
> Are all of Heaven that visits Helicon.
>
> Yet here, where never muse or god did haunt,
> Still may some nameless power of Nature stray,
> Pleased with the reedy stream's continual chant
> And purple pomp of these broad fields in May
> The shepherds meet him where he herds the kine,
> And careless pass him by whose is the gift divine.[1]

[1] From *Lyrics and Ballads.* By Margaret L. Woods (1889).

# THE DISENCHANTMENT OF THE ELIZABETHANS

THERE is a traditional estimate of Elizabethan literature. It has been established for us by a succession of brilliant historical writers—Taine, Green, Symonds, to name no others—and forms the foundation of every critical judgement of the age. Poetry, with whatever qualifications for the incalculable element of personality, is an expression of the life of a people; and when Gloriana sat in majesty, the English people had reached a momentous stage in its development. It had passed through the crucible. A new polity had built itself up on the ruins of mediæval ecclesiasticism and dynastic feud. A strong central government had maintained internal order, filled the Exchequer, and held fast against the combined onset of Roman intrigue and the maritime jealousy of Spain. And when the day of trial was over, and the last galleon of the Armada had cracked upon the inhospitable coasts of Ireland, the English folk found itself welded into a jubilant and united nation, conscious of its destiny, and ready to launch out into new adventures, earthly and spiritual alike. These are the spacious times, and of these what has come to be regarded as the characteristic Elizabethan poetry is the reflux. It is a belated Renaissance. A vigorous people lays aside its armour and its chill fears, and enters into the full inheritance of European civilisation, itself enriched by the realisation of its continuity with far-off and splendid origins in Greece and Rome. Ardent minds are athirst for form and colour, for passion and story, and for all the delightful circumstance of life. It is all tumbled into song, a song full of luxuriance, even of wantonness. The time for discipline, by balance, order and proportion, is not yet. Marlowe is typical, with his 'brave translunary things', his excess of sensuousness, his riot of golden words, the constant strain of his heroes to grasp more than is given to poor humanity of the lust of the eyes, the pride of knowledge, the pride of life, the craving for

> One thought, one grace, one wonder at the least,
> Which into words no virtue can digest.

And in the wake of Marlowe comes the whole of the earlier Elizabethan drama, hasty in workmanship, often crude in its popular appeal, but ranging widely over the literatures for its material, and filling the ear with a pompous rhetoric and the eye with a glittering spectacle in the long processional pageant of its English histories. Most typical of all is Spenser, who takes the pseudo-epic of the Renaissance straight from the hands of Ariosto and Tasso, and turns it into a tapestry full of delicate iridescent hues, and of incongruous imagery, in which the personages of the classical Olympus stray happily among the settings of Arthurian romances, and the abstractions of mediæval allegory lend themselves to the exposition of Elizabethan ideals of statecraft and churchmanship. *The Faerie Queene*, indeed, is by itself a mirror of the characteristic Elizabethan outlook, as it shows itself through the temperament of a man of genius, a little removed from the centre of the bustling scene. It has the formlessness, the comprehensiveness, the abundant and probing curiosity, the almost childish delight in the decorative surface of things, the deeply stirred national sentiment taking shape in that odd personal cult of a wholly idealised and transfigured Elizabeth. Spenser with his exquisite feeling both for physical and for moral beauty, Spenser with his easy mastery of fluent and melodious narrative, Spenser with his complete lack of that structural sense which is fundamental to the finest art, has contributed more than anyone else to fix for us our dominant conception of the Elizabethan temper. He holds the secret of its magic, and of its excess. You will remember that Landor, one of the most catholic of readers, could never taste Spenser. Landor, unlike Spenser, had learnt from classicism its deeper lessons of restraint, of symmetry, of the avoidance of superfluous ornament.

Elizabethanism then is sensuous, comprehensive, extravagant, disorderly, thirsty for beauty, abounding in the zest of life. There is much of truth here; but it is not the whole truth. You cannot sum up a whole age in a single formula, and I want to-day to call your attention to certain aspects of Elizabethan life and Elizabethan writing, the study of which may bring some qualification to this main impression of an ungirt and garlanded adolescence. In the first place I will ask you, without departing from the notion of Elizabethan literature as primarily an attempt to appropriate and acclimatise the tradition of insolent Greece and haughty Rome, to think for a moment in this connection, not so much of Spenser, as of that other fine poet, Samuel Daniel. Daniel, like Spenser, is a scholar and a classicist; to him too, in his own beautiful phrase, Apollo is 'the clear-eyed rector of the holy hill'. He has the same high sense, which marks all the greater Elizabethans, of the exalted function of poetry in life; of the special function of the English poet, to build up an edifice of English letters, proportioned to the place of Englishmen in the world.

> Or should we careless come behind the rest
>     In power of words, that go before in worth;
> When as our accent's equal to the best,
>     Is able greater wonders to bring forth,
> When all that ever hotter spirits expressed
>     Comes better'd by the patience of the North?

There is criticism and self-criticism in these lines. The 'patience of the North' is exactly what Daniel brings in qualification of the characteristic abandon of the Renaissance. Set him beside Spenser and his fellows, and you will see that he wears his rue with a difference. The gentle clarity of his verse at its best shows temperance where they are fervent; perhaps it is a little dull where they are exciting. And what Daniel is looking for in the ancients is

184

not so much the lust of the eyes and the pride of life, as the wisdom of life, that discipline of the heart and character which the Elizabethan found more readily than we do in the writings of the moralist and biographer Plutarch. It is the burden of his noble lines to the Countess of Cumberland, to whom he recalls, for she knows it, that—

> unless above himself he can
> Erect himself, how poor a thing is man.

And how turmoiled they are that level lie
  With earth, and cannot lift themselves from thence;
    That never are at peace with their desires,
But work beyond their years, and even deny
  Dotage her rest, and hardly will dispense
    With death; that when ability expires,
      Desire lives still, so much delight they have,
      To carry toil and travail to the grave.

Whose ends you see, and what can be the best
  They reach unto, when they have cast the sum
    And reckonings of their glory, and you know,
This floating life hath but this port of rest,
  *A heart prepared, that fears no ill to come.*

It will help to keep a true perspective, if we remember that the influence of Daniel upon contemporary writers was only second to that of Spenser himself, and also that, when Elizabethan poetry came to be rediscovered more than a century ago, the consonance of temper between Daniel and Wordsworth proved no less striking than that between Spenser and Keats.

Daniel's verses have already touched the theme of the instability of human reckonings. Life is a floating bark. That is a lesson with which this ebullient Elizabethan age was only too often brought face to face. After all, it was an age of transition, of reconstruction, as we call it. An old order had broken up. An old nobility was reluctantly losing its traditional privileges. A new one was establishing itself upon the basis of public service, and, what was less desirable, upon court favour. In all ages of reconstruction, there must be many who feel that the times are out of joint. The world was open for the adventurous; but there were disappointed adventurers, and there were men who were not prepared to accept some of the conditions which made adventure possible. This aspect of things also finds its reflection in the literature. For example, there were the recusants. It is not for me to consider here how far an administration, not yet secure from foreign aggression, is justified in disregarding the claims of toleration, in the interests of national security. In any case it was not a problem with which Elizabethan thought much concerned itself. Nor do I wish to ask how far Jesuit casuistry drew a defensible dividing line between conscientious objection and treason. The fact remains that, as the conflict with Spain and the Papacy hardened, there did come into existence a body of dispossessed and disinherited Englishmen, ruined in their estates by the oppressive recusancy fines, driven abroad to eat the bitter bread of exile, or called upon by their consciences to live the life of hunted creatures in their own land

as members of the English mission. Many of these
were men of birth and education, scholars and
poets, well fitted to take their share in the work of
the state, or to shine, like others their kinsmen, in
the masks and tilts at court. Do you know the
story, symbolical enough, of Thomas Pound? He
was a gentleman of Hampshire, a Catholic who
wore his religion lightly, a Gray's Inn lawyer, and
a famous dancer. One day he was called upon to
lead the revels at Christmas in the presence of
Elizabeth. He capered and pirouetted in a gal-
liard to the admiration of all beholders. When he
stopped he was hot and the presence-chamber was
draughty. The royal hand was extended; it removed a cap from no less an head than that of the
Earl of Leicester, and placed it upon Pound's.
Thomas Pound was at the top of his fame. He was
then bidden to repeat his performance. In so
doing he unfortunately stumbled and fell. Nothing,
of course, could be funnier to an English audience.
The maids of honour giggled. But the royal
countenance was overcast. 'Get up, you ox!', said
the Virgin Queen. And as he rose, the sudden
thought flashed through Pound, 'Sic transit gloria
mundi'. He made the sweeping bow of a courtier,
left the presence and the palace, turned to religion,
shortly became a recusant and a Jesuit, and spent
the greater part of his remaining forty-six years in
prison or under strict domiciliary supervision. Long
afterwards, we find him writing to that other
famous masker, Sir Christopher Hatton, to beg for

some trifling amelioration of his confinement at Bishop's Stortford, on the ground of a revel in which, as Hatton would remember, he had represented Mercury before the Queen at Kenilworth.

Into the souls of such men as Thomas Pound the iron entered, and their expression, when they happened to be poets, of the bitterness, or it might be the nothingness, of life, must not be left out of account as a factor in the total sum of Elizabethan letters. Pound was not a poet, or rather he was an extremely bad poet. But I can illustrate my point from the writings of another Jesuit of the same type, Father Robert Southwell. I do not think that Southwell was a very great poet either, although he had a considerable contemporary reputation. But he is at any rate characteristically Elizabethan in his fluency, his extravagances of expression, his accumulation of fantastic imagery. Only he is not jubilant; his turbulence is no overflow of superabundant and pagan vitality. Southwell writes always in the imminent shadow of death, which for him will be life well lost, and with that haunting sense of the fleetingness of all worldly goods, which in our literature is a mediæval rather than a Renaissance note.

> Ah life! sweet drop, drowned in a sea of sours,
>   A flying good, posting to doubtful end,
> Still losing months and years, to gain few hours,
>   Fain time to have and spare, yet forced to spend;
>     Thy growth, decrease, a moment all thou hast;
>     That gone, ere known; the rest to come or past.

## The Disenchantment of the Elizabethans

Ah life! the maze of countless straying ways,
  Open to erring steps and strewed with baits,
To wind weak senses into endless strays,
  Aloof from virtue's rough unbeaten straights,
    A flower, a play, a blast, a shade, a dream,
    A living death, a never-turning stream.

Or again, with greater simplicity and directness of utterance,

Continually at my bed's head
  A hearse doth hang, which doth me tell,
That I ere morning may be dead,
  Though now I feel myself full well:
    But yet, alas! for all this, I
    Have little mind that I must die.

The gown which I do use to wear,
  The knife wherewith I cut my meat,
And eke that old and ancient chair
  Which is my only usual seat;
    All these do tell me I must die,
    And yet my life amend not I.

My ancestors are turned to clay,
  And many of my mates are gone;
My youngers daily drop away,
  And can I think to 'scape alone?
    No, no, I know that I must die,
    And yet my life amend not I.

To Southwell's verses let me add those of Chidiock
Tichborne, who died for his share in the Babington
plot. They are said to have been written in the
Tower, on the night before his execution.

My prime of youth is but a frost of cares,
  My feast of joy is but a dish of pain,
My crop of corn is but a field of tares,
  And all my good is but vain hope of gain;
    The day is past, and yet I saw no sun,
    And now I live, and now my life is done.

My tale was heard, and yet it was not told,
  My fruit is fallen, and yet my leaves are green,
My youth is spent, and yet I am not old,
  I saw the world, and yet I was not seen;
    My thread is cut, and yet it is not spun,
    And now I live, and now my life is done.

I sought my death, and found it in my womb,
  I looked for life, and saw it was a shade,
I trod the earth, and knew it was my tomb,
  And now I die, and now I was but made;
    The glass is full, and now my glass is run,
    And now I live, and now my life is done.

It is not only in the writings of the recusants that this note of disillusion emerges; it is a constant undersong in the full strain of court poetry itself. I am not thinking of the mere palinode, in which the tired or disappointed amorist turns to woo the black instead of the fair, or renounces the monotony of his love-plaints for a bout of irony or railing. That is another affair altogether, a mere change of mood or pose, such as has been part of the convention of romantic love poetry since first the troubadours of Provence fixed the type. The heart of the amorist is unchanged. The disenchantment which sometimes fell upon the Elizabethans went deeper. There was a career for the adventurous at the court of Gloriana. A country lad might hope to come to London, like a Ralegh or a Hatton, with the price of half a dozen of his father's manors upon his back, and win his way, with a ready wit, or a skill in the dance, or sheer good looks, to a dazzling eminence of royal favour. But it was easier to climb those slippery slopes than to maintain a firm footing upon them. Beneath the superficial glamour, the struggle for existence was fierce. Perhaps this is common to courts. But there was a particularly queer streak in the Tudor composition, and Elizabeth was always a capricious and at heart an icy mistress. History is strewn with the ruins of her favourites; Oxford, Ralegh, Essex. Sidney was more fortunate, in his early death and unimpaired renown. And let us confirm the verdict of history by the contemporary judgement of Sir John Harington. Harington was in many ways a typical butterfly of the court. He was a godson of Elizabeth, who, to do her credit, never forgot the services of his family during her years of tribulation. He had a pretty wit, and sprinkled the court with epigrams, too topical, alas, in their allusions, to afford us much amusement to-day. He translated Ariosto, beginning, it is said, with one of the less discreet cantos for the edification of the maids of honour, and finishing the rest as a penance imposed by the Queen. He created another scandal with his *Metamorphosis of Ajax*, which has a pun in its title, and is in substance a compound of shrewd hygienic common sense and of humour which was always risky and

which the lapse of time has made somewhat un-
savoury. But these things were forgiven to one
whom Elizabeth probably did not take too seriously. In the end the butterfly did come very near
burning his wings, as a companion of Essex in his
disastrous Irish adventure. He got off with no
more than a few scathing words, and being at
heart a sensible man settled down in Somerset-
shire, with a wife and children whom he dearly
loved. Henceforth he delighted to call himself 'a
country knight that lives among clouted shoes, in
his frieze jacket and galloshes', and was content to
watch the further progress of Essex to rebellion
and the scaffold from a safe distance. Harington
kept a diary or note-book, in which he recorded
incidents of his life, side by side with philosophic
reflections upon the experience which it had brought
him. It begins while he was still a courtier, and
this is his view of the court—

In August I was much troubled at sundry grievances
from divers men in high states; but envy doth haunt many,
and breed jealousy. I will bid adieu to good company, and
leave sueing and seeking at court; for if I have no more
friends nor better at Heaven's court than at this, I shall
begin to think somewhat of brief damnation.

And again,

I have spent my time, my fortune, and almost my
honesty, to buy false hope, false friends, and shallow praise;
and be it remembered, that he who casteth up this reckoning
of a courtly minion, will set his sum like a fool at the end,
for not being a knave at the beginning.

And again,

> I see some men who love gaming, some men who love
> wenching, some men who love wine, and some who love
> trenchering. These oft find an empty purse, running reins,
> an aching head, and grumbling guts. Now what findeth he
> who loveth the 'pride of life', the court's vanity, ambition's
> puff-ball? In sooth, no more than empty words, grinning
> scoff, watching nights and fawning days. *Felix quem
> faciunt aliena pericula cautum!*

These trenchant comments were of course intended
for Harington's private self-direction. But he had
always the gift of fearless and agreeable imperti-
nence, and he records how, when he heard that
Philip of Spain had been eaten by lice while living,
he reflected,

> God grant me no further ambition than to be eaten by
> worms when I am dead!

'And this', he adds, 'I said to the Queen.'

I come back to Spenser, our most exemplary
Elizabethan, outside the dramatists, whom I must
leave alone. Spenser soon quitted the ways of the
court. The vision of England in *The Faerie Queene*,
as already suggested, is a remote one, veiled by all
that separates London from 'the green alders by
the Mulla's shore'. And the final tragedy of
Spenser's life was even more primitive and external
than the outcome of a court disappointment. But
his *Colin Clout's Come Home Again*, written after
a brief visit to England, yields curious echoes of
Harington's complaints. He is not blind to the
brilliance of all that he has seen. How could he be,

being Spenser. He hymns the peace and plenty, contrasting so with the 'nightly bordrags' and the 'hues and cries' of Ireland. He hymns the presence of Cynthia, the 'dreaded Dread', whose 'name recorded I will leave for ever', and the nymphs that cluster about her throne, and the shepherds that 'blow their pipes around, her name to glorify'. But his last word is one of criticism. Why did he come back to Kilcolman? Because the court was no place for a silly shepherd.

> Where each one seeks with malice and with strife,
> To thrust down other into foul disgrace,
> Himself to raise: and he doth soonest rise
> That best can handle his deceitful wit,
> In subtle shifts, and finest sleights devise.... 
> For highest looks have not the highest mind,
> Nor haughty words most full of highest thoughts:
> But are like bladders blowen up with wind,
> That being pricked do vanish into noughts.
> Even such is all their vaunted vanity,
> Nought else but smoke, that fumeth soon away;
> Such is their glory that in simple eye
> Seem greatest, when their garments are most gay.
> So they themselves for praise of fools do sell,
> And all their wealth for painting on a wall;
> With price whereof they buy a golden bell,
> And purchase highest rooms in bower and hall:
> Whiles single truth and simple honesty
> Do wander up and down despised of all;
> Their plain attire such glorious gallantry
> Disdains so much, that none them in do call.

Disillusionment, baffled ambitions, unavailing regrets, Coleridge's

194

## The Disenchantment of the Elizabethans

Sense of past youth, and manhood come in vain,
And genius given, and knowledge won in vain;

You will find plenty of all this in the writings of the
court poets, if you look below the surface, where it
mingles oddly enough with the graces and conceits,
the careless rapture, of their official ditties. Take that
very great man, Sir Walter Ralegh, a typical Elizabethan, with his inexhaustible vitality, his personal
arrogance, the extravagance of a Captain of the
Guard, the imaginative political outlook of a maker
of empires. Some of the best of Ralegh went into
his poetry. Very little of it is left to us, but that little
reveals fundamental brain-work, a power of con-
centrated phrasing, which was only too rare among
his contemporaries. Elizabethan commendatory
verse is generally flat and formal, but how greatly
Ralegh's sonnet to the author of the *Faerie Queene* is
planned.

Methought I saw the grave, where Laura lay,
    Within that temple, where the vestal flame
Was wont to burn, and passing by that way,
    To see that buried dust of living fame,
Whose tomb fair Love and fairer Virtue kept,
    All suddenly I saw the Faerie Queene.
At whose approach the soul of Petrarch wept,
    And from thenceforth those graces were not seen,
For they this Queene attended, in whose stead
    Oblivion laid him down on Laura's hearse.
Hereat the hardest stones were seen to bleed,
    And groans of buried ghosts the heavens did pierce;
        Where Homer's spright did tremble all for grief,
    And cursed th' access of that celestial thief.

'Oblivion laid him down on Laura's hearse'—
what a magnificent conceit! Ralegh wrote a long
poem to Elizabeth, as from the Shepherd of the
Ocean to Cynthia. He read it to Spenser in Ireland
during 1589. Other writers refer to it as 'a fine
and sweet invention' and in a 'vein most lofty,
insolent, and passionate'. It was never printed and
was already lost by the middle of the seventeenth
century. But you can guess at the theme, with its
fine central image of the mistress swaying the hopes
and fears of the lover, as the moon sways the ebb
and flow of the tides. The lover is both shepherd
and mariner; the moon now rides remote and
inaccessible among the cloud drifts; now descends
to hang like a golden lamp upon the tree-tops, as
in that serene Latmian night, when Diana came
down to sleep with Endymion. We do not know
what Ralegh made of it; we should gladly know.
Spenser tells us that it was the music of 'the
summer's nightingale'. There is indeed among the
Hatfield manuscripts a set of verses in Ralegh's
handwriting, headed 'The 11th and last booke of
the Ocean to Scinthia'. This is, however, quite
clearly no part of the original poem, but an after-
piece of different inspiration. Some think that it
was written after the death of Elizabeth while
Ralegh was imprisoned in the Tower, as a supposed traitor against James. But I am sure that
this is a misconception. The Queen is not dead;
but a great rift has come between her and Ralegh,
something which he can only regard as a final and

irretrievable breach of a twelve years' adoration. The date must be that of Ralegh's first imprisonment in the Tower, after his marriage with Elizabeth Throckmorton in 1592, and the tone is in keeping with his singular letters and behaviour of that time. It is the longest of his poems which we possess, and a difficult one to read, since it is evidently a rough draft, with many imperfect rhymes and unfinished stanzas, and obscurities of expression which revision would perhaps have removed. But it is full of vivid, pregnant images and of a haunting music. Here is still the nightingale's voice, though muted.

> With youth is dead the hope of Love's return,
>    Who looks not back to hear our after cries;

or again:

> On Sestus' shore, Leander's late resort,
>    Hero hath left no lamp to guide her love.

Or of the workings of love in the mind of a man,

> Even as the moisture in each plant that grows;
>    Even as the sun unto the frozen ground;
> Even as the sweetness to th' incarnate rose;
>    Even as the centre in each perfect round.

And it is written in a mood of the deepest dejection. The deserted lover sits before the ashes of dead fires, brooding over the memories of golden days gone beyond recall. He has served and worshipped in vain, and all his past joys and sorrows are alike dust. He is to be 'th' example in love's story'. All his songs have availed him nothing.

> She cares not for thy praise, who knows not theirs;
>     It's now an idle labour, and a tale
> Told out of time, that dulls the hearer's ears,
>     A merchandise whereof there is no sale.
>
> Leave them, or lay them up with thy despairs!
>     She hath resolved, and judged thee long ago.
> Thy lines are now a murmuring to her ears.

Of course it is all rather extravagant. Ralegh was destined to shine in the sun of court favour again, for long enough before his final tragedy began. But to be deeply down-cast by a comparative trifle was always in keeping with his pressing, impetuous temperament, which brooked delay as hardly as failure. He says himself,

> At middle day my sun seemed under land,
>     When any little cloud did it obscure.

And of course it is largely a pose. Ralegh was not really in love with Elizabeth; that was only the usual and rather wearisome convention, although he carries it off well. This does not mean that the melancholy and the regret were unreal. They were genuine enough, but what underlay them was only the shipwreck of Ralegh's ambitions, not of his affections, which were set firmly upon Elizabeth Throckmorton. In most of the rest of Ralegh's verse, in the denunciations of *The Lie*, for example, the same note of criticism upon life and its conditions is predominant; always powerful in its utterance, generally noble in its sentiment, but occasionally touched with mere railing. He is never ready to accept, save perhaps in those last

years, when the irrepressible hopes were beginning
to grow frail, until they resigned themselves in the
lines said to have been written on the night before
his execution, which form so fit a prelude to the high
bearing of his end.

> Even such is Time, which takes in trust
> Our youth, our joys, and all we have,
> And pays us but with age and dust;
> Who in the dark and silent grave,
> When we have wandered all our ways,
> Shuts up the story of our days:
> And from which earth, and grave, and dust,
> The Lord shall raise me up, I trust.

Herein the rumoured atheist, at the close of his long
voyage, casts anchor beside the Jesuit Southwell.

The reaction against courtly life, with its perilous
achievements and its fatal uncertainties, finds its
echo in others besides Ralegh; other broken
favourites and baffled aspirants. The note is not
always one of rebellion or of despair. There are
men who are still captains of their souls; they have
won their way, by thorny paths, to the same
philosophy, which Daniel learnt so easily from the
books of his classical teachers. One of these is
Sir Edward Dyer, a lifelong servant of Elizabeth,
but content with the kingdom of his own mind.

> I see how plenty suffers oft,
>   And hasty climbers soon do fall;
> I see that those which are aloft
>   Mishap doth threaten most of all;
>     They get with toil, they keep with fear:
>     Such cares my mind could never bear.

199

> Some have too much, yet still do crave;
>   I little have, and seek no more.
> They are but poor, though much they have,
>   And I am rich with little store.
>     They poor, I rich; they beg, I give.
>     They lack, I leave; they pine, I live.
>
> I laugh not at another's loss;
>   I grudge not at another's gain;
> No worldly waves my mind can toss;
>   My state at one doth still remain.
>     I fear ro foe, I fawn no friend;
>     I loathe not life, nor dread my end.

There are others again who, like Sir John Harington, withdraw from the world, or are fain to do so; the Earl of Oxford, making his 'doubtful choice' between

> A kingdom, or a cottage, or a grave;

the Earl of Essex, one of the most brilliant and the most unfortunate of them all.

> Happy were he could finish forth his fate
>   In some unhaunted desert, most obscure
> From all societies, from love and hate
>   Of worldly folk; then might he sleep secure;
> Then wake again, and give God ever praise,
>   Content with hips and haws and bramble-berry;
> In contemplation spending all his days,
>   And change of holy thoughts to make him merry;
>     Where, when he dies, his tomb may be a bush,
>     Where harmless robin dwells with gentle thrush.

We must all have noticed how this hymning of content forms a persistent burden in the full harmony of Elizabethan song; always there beneath the flutes and bugles of its most triumphant mood. It answers to something deep in the Elizabethan consciousness. It lies at the heart of the enduring popularity of pastoral poetry. No doubt the pastoral was itself part of the classical and Renaissance tradition, handed down from Theocritus and Virgil, through Baptista Mantuanus and his Italian fellows. But it is characteristic of the great conventions of literature that they lend themselves to reshaping by every age in turn. And so the Elizabethans, in a time when city life was already beginning to bear something of its modern oppression, fashioned for themselves a new Arcadia of running brooks and enamelled meads and simple lives, where the shepherd boys piped as though they should never be old, and disheartened ambition might lay aside its burden and find its peace.

There are other topics upon which I should have liked to dwell. I should have liked to say something of the Elizabethan sonneteers; of that old literary convention of love as a service and a tyranny—*Ecce Deus fortior me, qui veniens dominabitur mihi*—which took shape as the leisurely life of settled courts, with its time for literature and its place for women, emerged in twelfth-century France from the rough and tumble of the Dark Ages; of the new form invented for that convention by the genius of Petrarch; of its westward drift, partly direct from Italy, and partly through such

French disciples as Marot and Ronsard, to Surrey
and Sidney and Spenser himself; of the balance in
the English sonneteers, even the greatest of them,
between the trappings of the convention and the
frequent sincerity of feeling which those trappings
partly conceal, and of the general relation between
form and matter in lyric poetry which is thereby
illustrated. And over against that vogue of the
sonnet, re-echoing as it does the Spenserian epic
in many of its characteristic beauties and weak-
nesses, I should have liked to put the simpler and
no less lucid songs of the madrigalists and lutenists,
and to trace in them, side by side with the Renaissance influences, a continuity of a clear English
tradition flowing direct from the Middle Ages, and
in close relation to that unrivalled supremacy of
contemporary English music which modern research is doing so much to reveal. Above all I
should have liked to point out how transitory, after
all, was the Spenserian influence in poetry, how
inadequate were the pupils of the Master to wear
his mantle, and how, even as *The Faerie Queene*
came from the press, John Donne was beginning
to write that new and intimate lyric, with some
kinship perhaps to Ralegh and a little to Marlowe,
but none whatever to Spenser, which was destined
more than anything else to transform the poetic
outlook of the next generation.

The personality of John Donne is as much the
dominating single influence in the poetry of the
first quarter of the seventeenth century, as is the

personality of Spenser in that of the last quarter of
the sixteenth. It was a little slow in establishing
itself, because it was not Donne's habit to print his
verses, and the slow processes of manuscript transmission delayed their full effect upon disciples
and imitators for at least a generation. But the best
and most characteristic of those verses almost
certainly date from the reign of Elizabeth, and from
the beginning they reveal a temper in revolt from
the facilities of the Spenserians and the sonneteers,
an instinct to have done with the trappings and to
find as direct an utterance as possible for the
exaltations and revulsions of one who, in the ardour
and self-confidence of youth, feels that he has 'seen
things bare to the buff'. Poetry, for Donne, shall be
a thing not of jewelry and enamel work, but of
fantastically wrought iron; he will purge, not
decorate, his soul.

> Grief brought to numbers cannot be so fierce,
> For he tames it, that fetters it in verse.

It is a perturbed world into which you pass from
the serenity of Spenser. 'The words of Mercury
are harsh after the songs of Apollo.' They are
contradictory and often perverse moods that Donne
will express, full of the self-torturings of a philosophic amorist, caught in the obvious snares of his
own body. But they bring a new note of sincerity
into English song, a note which, it need hardly be
said, Donne's own disciples were in their turn,
quick to lose. Well, the complicated mentality of

## The Disenchantment of the Elizabethans

John Donne is no subject for the fag-end of a lecture. I am conscious that Time's winged chariot is hurrying by, and perhaps I have said enough to illustrate my main theme of the complexity of Elizabethan poetry, and of the cross-currents which have to be borne in mind in attempting to form any complete and balanced estimate of its contribution to our literature.

# APPENDIX

# THE COURT OF VENUS

Two fragments of *The Courte of Venus* are preserved in print. One, formerly in the Bright and Britwell collections, is now in the Folger Shakespeare Library at Washington. It is sign. A of a small octavo in black-letter type of long primer size. A title-page, without imprint or date, occupies the recto of the first leaf; the verso is blank. The other leaves are foliated from 2 to 8, and contain a narrative prologue in verse and twelve lyrics, the last of which is incomplete. The running-title for ff. 2ᵛ–4 is 'The (the) Prologue | of Venus' and thereafter 'The (the) Court | of Venus'. The text is in single columns, except on ff. 6ᵛ–7ᵛ, where parts are in double columns. The title-page, reproduced in facsimile on p. 209, has a woodcut border (McKerrow and Ferguson 107), which is also found, less damaged, in Sir Thomas Elyot's *Castel of Health*, printed by Thomas Marsh in 1561. The type of the fragment is used in John Fitzherbert's *Boke of Husbandry* (1558), John Hall's *Courte of Vertu* (1565) and in the side-notes to Augustine Marlorat's *Catholike Exposition of S. Mathewe* (1570). All three were printed by Marsh, and it is a reasonable inference that the fragment also came from his press, later than 1561 and not much, if at all, later than 1565. I am much indebted to Dr McKerrow and Mr Strickland Gibson for help in making this identification. Some manuscript entries on ff. 4, 5 and 6, one of which may be either a date or a press-mark, have thrown no further light. Of the lyrics, the Egerton MS. of Wyatt has (ii), (vii) and (xi); the Devonshire MS. has (i), (ii), (vii) and (xi), not in all cases definitely ascribed to Wyatt, together with some lines (ed. Foxwell, i. 324), which seem to be a shorter version of (x); Tottel has (ii), (iv) and (xi). So far as I know, (iii), (v), (vi), (viii), (ix) and (xii) do not occur elsewhere. Miss Foxwell (i. 357) printed (iii) from the *Court*, but unfortunately gave the

207

title-page (ii. 175) as reading *Courte of Venice*. The texts printed as from the *Court* by Mrs C. C. Stopes in *Shakespeare's Industry* (1916) are in several cases, as she seems to have suspected at the last moment, really taken from the sources already known. My acknowledgments are due to the Trustees of the Folger Library and to their Supervisor of Research, Dr J. Q. Adams, for their courtesy in allowing me to give a full reprint for the first time from a photostat. I have added such variants as are available from the *Boke of Balettes*, as printed by Professors Griffith and Law. They are probably incomplete, as several lines of the recovered fragments are illegible.

A second fragment of the *Court*, from the Douce collection, is in the Bodleian (formerly Douce Fr. 92$^b$, now Douce g. 3). It consists of signs. E and F from another small octavo, but the last leaf is missing. The foliation is from xxxi to xlv. The running-title of the first leaf is ' The court of | Venus'; that of the others 'The pylgryms | Tale', except on one page, where 'Venus' stands in error for 'Tale'. The type is black-letter of pica size. Clearly the fragment cannot have come from the same volume as the Folger one. Colonel Isaac kindly tells me that the nearest type is his ii. 10, used by T. Gybson in 1535. Gybson printed to 1539, and apparently again in 1553. A *Court* might conceivably have appeared, even with a poem by Wyatt in it, during the earlier period. But secular verse does not seem to have been in Gybson's line, and the type may have passed into other hands. There is nothing to link it with Henry Sutton. On f. xxxi are the end of one lyric and the whole of another, some phrases of which recur in a piece of Wyatt's (ed. Foxwell, i. 340) preserved in the Devonshire MS. and by Tottel. The rest of the fragment is occupied by *The pylgrymse tale*, which remains incomplete. The full contents are reprinted by Furnivall (2 *Chaucer Soc.* xiii, 77, 127), and I have only given the lyrics here.

THE

Courte of
Uenus. Newly
and diligently cor-
rected with many pro-
per Ballades newly
amended, and also
added therbnto
which haue not
before bene
imprin=
ted.

TITLE-PAGE OF FOLGER FRAGMENT

# FOLGER FRAGMENT

The Courte of Venus. Newly and diligently corrected ⟨Title:
with many proper Ballades newly amended, and also added *vide*
thervnto which haue not before bene imprinted.  ⟨p. 209⟩

## The Prologue. ⟨Fol. 2⟩

I N the moneth of may when the new tender grene
    Hath smothly couered the ground that was bare
    Poudred with flours, so wel be sene
    I would haue brought my hart out of care
And as I walked in the wood so fayre
Thycke of grasse among the floures swete
And many a holsome herbe fayre vnder the fete.

    I heard one hunt, me thought it did blow
In a great horne of stryfe sowne
At the roote of the heart, as farre as I could know
Toward the cry I had me fast bowne
And at the last, for weary I sat me downe
Thynking a whyle to take my restyng
The houndes were gone out of my hearing.

    And for that I know my selfe to be alone
And sodeinly my grefe, I beganne to complayne
Me thought I had good place, my selfe to mone
And ease my hart of myne owne payne
Besechyng Venus to lose me out of chayne
I was so fast and sure stong through the hart
Wyth the fyry chayne, that I could not start.

    And as I was making my complaint
Of my true seruyce to my lady deare
And how nothing I was repentaunt
Saue to her presence, I was not taken nere
Genius came and asked me what cheare
Who is with Venus put in such trust
That lyke to dye for loue, confesse them he must.

2 1 1

Venus knew I had a woful hart
And wher we thus content she knoweth her relefe
To me therfore she send her owne clarke

⟨Fol. 2ᵛ⟩

To slacke my sorowes, and helpe me of my gryefe
That was so far in daunger and myschiefe
For whether I would, she knew I durst not speake
Whych caused my hart in sonder to breake.

I layd my head betwixt my life and death
Vpon his kne, and what he said I heard
And by that time I scarsly drew my breath
But hard his tale or I answered
It hath bene pity, him to haue disturbed
Oftentimes he bad, that I should leaue my wo
and sayd of my dysease ther were fyue hundreth mo.

He bad therfore that I wyth pen and ynke
Redy wyth wryting should make my complaynt
Ther shalbe a redresse, soner then ye thinke
And bad no more that my heare should raynt
And of our bylles, he sayd he would none want
Of them he thought to haue good comfort
And would present him selfe iꞧ Venus court.

For she entendeth, and that is in al hast
To surmount the parlyament as fast as can be done
And Iupiter himselfe within this day past
Hath commaunded Marcury for to be gone
Vpon his message, some cal him Stylbone
With his commission also for to compel
Mynos to come, the iudge of dreful hel.

To the mount of Cethro, wher Venus doth dwel
The preparement made is so farre exceding
That if such triumphe no storyes doth tel
That is aboue al other so farre transcending
And for the whyle, she had me by copying
Of these complaynes which doth folow

⟨Fol. 3⟩     And after that I should know the matter thorow

212

The whole fashion of euery thing
He would me send therfore we must be gone
Of matters determined, aswel as of the meting
But I besought him, or euer I were alone
That of Venus court he would interpret the fashion
Some thing to make but he would not consent
Tyl it were concluded by the parliament.

But thus farre he sayd he durst report
That loue without charitie, should be put downe
Nor periured persons, should no more resort
Vnto the court of Venus doth frowne
When the religion hath them bowne
And to Diana them selfe hath also sworne
And yet through Heccates in her court be borne.

Whom the Poets cal the gods of courtesy
That now is in so great dyspleasure
And like to be expelled for his baudry
Whych hath done mischiefe out of measure
Ipocrysye is spyed for al his treasure
That he spedeth as wel as the false foxe
As that in armes, had many a bloudy boxe.

And Venus intendeth Diana to compel
For to supporte vnder the coulour of chastitie
No more in asking, but to expel
Out of her retynew inconueniently
For whose supporting she is had in ielousye
And thus he went and bad me farewel
And at another tyme he would me more tel.

And therfore I must (my reader) intreat
Desyryng you hartely to be content          ⟨Fol. 3ᵛ⟩
For though I haue not, I wyl not forget
To describe the court, I wil deligent
And at the end of this complaynt set it
But I as nothing of myne induction
Wyl once report of Genius instruction.

213

And here foloweth, wherin you may rede
To the court of Venus a greate nomber
Their harts they say be as heauy as lead
Their sorowful wo, I am sure you wil tender
For if that I were mayden vncumber
And had such myght as she hath mone
Out of their payne they should be lettin gone.

¶ Thus endeth the prologue, and hereafter foloweth the new court
of Venus.

⟨ i ⟩

MY penne take payne a lytle space
to folow the thing that doth me chase
and hath in hold, my hart so sore
And when thou hast this brought to passe:
My pen I praye the wryte no more.

Remember how thou hast oft pleased
And al my sorowes also eased
But now vnknowen, I knew before
That wher I trust I am deceyued
And yet my pen thou canst do no more.

A tyme thou hadst as other haue
To wryt whych way my hope to craue
That tyme is past, wythdraw therfore
⟨Seyng⟩ we doe lose and other saue
⟨Fol. 4⟩        As good leaue of, and wryt no more,

i 3 hath in] *om.*   6 how] *om.*   7 al] *om.*   14 ⟨Seyng⟩ Hens. The
Folger line is mutilated, but the restoration seems probable. *Devonshire*
has Syns.   14 and] let

## Appendix

And vse to worke another way
Not as ye would but as ye may
For els my life is past restore
and my desire is my decay
and yet my pen now wryt no more.

To loue in vaine whosoeuer shal
Of worldly payne it passeth al
As in like case, I find wherfore
To hold so fast, and yet to fal
Alas my pen now wryte no more.

Seyng thou hast taken payne this space
To folow that whych doth me chase
and hath in hold my hart so sore
And now to haue brought this to passe
My pen I pray the to wryt no more.

### Finis.

i 20] *om.*  21 shal] *om.*  25 Alas] Alak  26 Seyng] Syns  27 me] the
29 to haue brought this] thou hast this brought  30 to] *om.*

### ⟨ ii ⟩

M Y lute awake performe the last
Labour that thou and I shal wast,
and end that I haue new begone
For when this song, is gon and past
My lute be stil for I haue done

As to be heard wher eare is none
A⟨s⟩ lead to graue in a marble stone
My song may perse, heart as sone
Should we then syng, wepe or mone
No more my lute for I haue done.

ii 4 gon] sung    7 A⟨s⟩] Completed from *Egerton.*    7 a] *om.*
8 heart] her hart

215

The rocke doth not so cruelly
Repulse the waues continually
As she my sute and affection.

So that I am past al remedy
Wherby my lute and I haue done

Proud of the splen that thou hast shot
Of symple hart, through loues got
Vnkind although thou hast them won
Thinke not he hath his owne forgot
Although my lute and I haue done.

Vengeaunce may fal on such dysdayne
That maketh but game of earnest paine
Trow not alone vnder the sonne
Vngently to cause to louers plaine
Although my lute and I haue done

And then may chaunce the to repent
The time that thou hast lost and spent
To cause thy louer to sighe and sowne
Then shalt thou know beauty but lent
And wyshe and want as I haue done

My lute be stil this is the last
Labour that thou and I shal wast
And end that I haue begonne
Or when this song is song and past
My lute be stil for I haue done.

Finis.

ii 13 affection] effeccion    17 got] shot    19 owne] bow    23 Trow]
...true    24 to] the

〈 iii 〉

TO whom should I sue to ease my payne
To my mysters, nay nay certayne
For feare she should me then disdayne
I dare not sue, I dare not sue.

When I should speake to my mystres
In hope for to get redres
〈　.　.　.　.　.　〉
When I should speake, when I shold speake          〈Fol. 5〉

What hap had I that suffereth payne
And if I myght her grace attayne
Or els she would here me complayne
What hap had I, what hap had I.

I fly for feare to be espyed
Or of euil wil to be destroyed
The place wher I would faynest abyde
I fly for feare, I fly for feare.

Though I were bold who should me blame
Loue caused me to do the same
Wyth honesty it were no shame
Thouth I were bold, though I were bold.

And here an end, wyth ful glad wyl
In purpose for to serue her styl
And for to part thinke none yl
And here an end, and here an end.

Finis.

217

⟨ iv ⟩

DYsdaine me not without desert
   Nor leaue me not so sodeynly
   Sence wel ye wot that in my hart
I meane nothing but honesty
   Dysdayne me not

Refuse me not without cause why
Nor thynke me not to be vniust
Synce that by lot of fantasye
The careful knot nedes knyt I must.
   Refuse me not.

Mystrust me not though some therbe
That fayne would spot thy stedfastness
Beleue them not seyng that ye se
⟨Fol. 5ᵛ⟩    The profe is not as they expresse
   Mystrust me not.

   Forsake me not til I deserue
Nor hate me not til I swarue
⟨Destroy me not, tyll that I swerue⟩
For syth you knew what I entend,
   Forsake me not.

Dysdayne me not being your owne
Refuse me not that I am so true
Mystrust me not til al be knowen
Forsake me neuer for no new
   Disdayne me not.

Finis.

iv (variants from *Tottel*)  4 nothing] ye not  4 honesty] honestly
5 *om.*  9 The] This  10 *om.*  12 thy] my  13 seyng] sins  15 *om.*
17 swarue] offend  18 Added from *Tottel.*  19 For syth you knew]
But sins ye know  20 *om.*  21 being] that am  22 I] *om.* 24 neuer]
not, ne  25 *om.*

⟨ v ⟩

FOrtune what ayleth the
Thus for to banyshe me
Her company whom I loue best,
For to complayne me
Nothing auayleth me
Adew farewel this nights rest.

Her demure countenaunce
Her womanly countenaunce
Hath wounded me through Venus darte,
That I cannot refrayne me
Nother yet abstayne me
But nedes must loue her withal my hart.

Long haue I loued her
Oft haue I proued her
Yet alas through dysdayne
Nothyng regardyng me
Nor yet rewardeth me
But letteth me lye in mortal payne.

Yet shal I ⟨l⟩oue her still
Wythal my hart and wyl
Wher so euer I ryde or go                    ⟨Fol. 6⟩
My hart my seruyce
Afore al ladyes
Is hers al onely and no mo

She hath my hart and euer shal
In this terrestrial
What can she more of me require
Her whom I loue best
God send her good rest
And me hartely my whole desyre

Finis.

219

## Appendix

### ⟨ vi ⟩

I May by no meanes surmyse
My fantasy to resyst
But after the old gyse
To cal on had I wyst
And thought it to suffyce
That agayne I shal haue none
Yet can I not deuyse
To get agayne myne owne.

It is my hart that I haue lost
God send it me againe
I should it haue what euer it cost
Or els I am but slaine
I study day and night
And loud I cry and cal
To be deliuered quyte
From her that I am thral

And yet agaynst al right
Of force I must stil mone
For it doth passe my might
To get agayne myne owne. &c.

⟨Fol. 6ᵛ⟩

In tormentes I am torne
That no rest find I can
None so vnhappy borne
Sence that the world began
I aske but such corne
And such sede that was sowne
And yet though I had sworne
I cannot get my owne.

vi 20 Four lines omitted, with '&c' as an apology! The catchword
is 'in'.

220

## Appendix

But seyng that I cannot
Attayne my true desyre
Nor by no meane may not
Crepe out of the fyre
Geue ought of your owne
By reason that you should not
Let me to haue myne owne.

Finis,

### ⟨ vii ⟩

IF 'fantasy would fauour
As I deserue and shal
My loue my lady paramour
should loue me best of al

And if I not attayne
The grace that I desire
Then may I wel complayne
My seruyce and my hier

Fantasy knoweth how
To forbeare my true hart
If fantasye might auow
Wyth fayth to take part

But fantasy is frayle
And fletynge styl so fast
that faith may not preuail
To helpe me fyrst nor last

Since fantasy at his luste
Doth rule al by gesse
Wherto shoulde I put trust
In truth and stedfastnes.

221

## Appendix

Yet gladly would I please
That fantasy of my hart
That may me onely ease
and helpe my careful smart.

Therfore my lady deare
Let se your fantasy
to make some appeare
Of helpe and remedy

⟨Fol. 7⟩

For if ye be my frend
And vndertake my wo
My gryefe is at an end
If ye contynew so.

Els fantasy doth not ryght.
As I deserue and shal
To her day and night
To loue me best of al.

vii 22 That] The    27 some] some hope    35 her] haue her

### ⟨ viii ⟩

D Vring of payne and greuous smart
Hath brought me lowe & wōderous weake
that I cānot cōfort my hart
why sighest thou my hart & wil not breake

The sighes and plaintes are al in vaine
the teares that from thyne eyes doth leake
This life is death, this ioy is payne
Why syghest thou hart and wil not breake

Thou clymest to catche wher is no hold
Thou pullest the stringes that be to weake
Thy careful lyfe cannot be told
Why syghest thou hart and wyl not breake

222

## *Appendix*

The faythfuller thou dost endure
Lesse she regarded to heare the speke
And kyng pytye wyl the not cure
Why sighest thou hart and wil not breake.

As good thou were a sunder to ryue
As thus in thought thy selfe to breake
Better to dy then thus to lyue
Why syghest thou hart and wil not breake.

I pray the pytye shew redresse
Or els come death thy selfe awreake
And if thou fynd no gentlenesse
Syth no more, but hart thou breaket.

Finis.

⟨ ix ⟩

Now must I lern to faine                    ⟨Fol. 7ᵛ⟩
and do as other do
Seing no truth doth raine
That I may trust vnto
I was both true & playne
To one and to no mo
And vnto me againe
Alas she was not so.

Vnknowē againe my hart
Into my foes hand
and euer I could astart
Out of that careful band
Al the wyt I had
Could scace the knot vndo
This careful lyfe I had
For one that was no so.

223

## Appendix

The night right lōg & heuy
The dayes of my torment
The sighes continually
That thorow my hart wēt
My colour pale and wan
To her dyd playnly shewe
That I was her true man
And yet she thought not so

Out of her sight no pleasur
But to my hart gret paine
And teares out of measure
yᵗ out of mine eies did raine
Her absence was my death
For to depart her fro
And yet alas her fayth
Was fayned and not so.

Not the feuer quartayne
Doth halfe a man so shake
As dyd the wo and payne
That dayly dyd me take
No slepe could I nor rest
But tossyng to and fro
And wheras I loued best
Alas she did not so,

And seing it is my chaūce
My loue in vaine to wast
I am not in that daunce
The first nor yet the last
But wise he is by once
That can his foly know
To reuoke at once
Seyng she wyl no so.

Finis.

## Appendix

### ⟨ x ⟩

LOue whom you lyst and spare not
  Therwyth I am content
  Hate whom you lyst and spare not
For I am indyfferent

Do what you lyst and dread not
After your owne fantasye
Thynke what you lyst and feare not
For al is one with me.         ⟨Fol. 8⟩

For as for me I am not
Wauering as the wind
But euen as one that reketh not
Whych way you turne your mind

For in your loue I doubt not
But as one that reketh not
Whether you hate or hate not
Is least charge of my thought.

Wherfore I pray you forget not
But that I am wel content
To loue whom you list and spare not
For I am indyfferent

Finis.

x 3 you] ye    4 I] euen I    5 you] ye    8 with] to    12 you] ye
15 you] yon   16 Is least] In lest   16 thought] thou   19 you] ye

### ⟨ xi ⟩

MEruaile no more al tho
  The songes I sing do mone
  For other life then woe
I neuer proued none
And in my hart also
Is grauen with letters depe
And many thousands mo
The flouds of teares to wepe.

225

How may a man in smart
Find mater to reioyce
How may a woful hart
Set forth a pleasaunt voyce
Play who can that depart
In me must nedes appere
How fortune ouerthwart
⟨Doeth cause my morning chere.⟩

⟨Fol. 8ᵛ⟩ Perdye ther is no man
If he neuer saw syght
That parfectly tel can
The nature of the light
How should I than
That neuer tasted but soure
But do as I began
Continually to loure.

Such chaunce perchaunce may chaunce
To cause me chaunge my tune
And when such chaunce doth chaunce
Then shal I thanke fortune
And if such chaunce do chaunce
Perchaunce or it be long
For such a pleasant chaunce
To sing some pleasant song.

Finis.

xi 16 Added from *Egerton*.

⟨ xii ⟩

S Hal she neuer out of my mynd
Nor shal I neuer out of my payne
Alas her ioy doth so bind
For lacke of helpe now am I slayne

xii 2 my] this    3 ioy doth so bind] loue doth me so blinde    4 For lacke of] Except her    4 now am I] I am now

226

## Appendix

I neuer told her of my mynd
What payne I suffer for his sake
Alas what paynes myght I now find
That no displeasure with me she take

Yf I speake fayre she sayth I flatter
And if I dare not, I shal not spede
If I to her do wryte a letter
Then will she say she cannot rede.

Shal I dyspayre yet ⟨for al⟩ this
Nay nay my hart wil not do so
⟨I wold ones my swete hart kys
A thousand tymes to bynd more wo

I am abashed when I shuld speake
Alas I can not my mind expresse
Yt maketh my hart in peces breake
To se her louing gentelnes   Finis⟩

xii 6 his] her   7 paynes] meanes   9 flatter] *om.?*   10 dare] do
11 do] to 13 ⟨for al⟩ Uncertain through a hole in the paper, and
restored from *B.B.*   15–20 Added from *B.B.*, but *C. of V.* has
catchword 'I'.

227

# DOUCE FRAGMENT

⟨ *a* ⟩

⟨Fol. xxxi⟩

which had me in the snare
of pensyue thought and payn.

She saw that faithfully
I dyd my hert resynge
to take it gentylly.
she dyd nothing repyn.

Wherfore away all payn.
for now I am right sure
pyte in hir doth rayn
that hath my hert in cur.  Finis

⟨ *b* ⟩

¶ Dryuen by dissyr to set affection.
a great way alas aboue my degre
chosen I am I thinke by election.
to couet that thing that will not be.

I serue in loue not lyke to sped.
I loke alas a lytell to hye.
agaynst my will I do in ded.
couet that thing that will not be.

My fanzy alas doth me so bynd
that I can se no remedy
but styll to folow my folych mind.
and couet that thing that wyll not be.

⟨Fol. xxxiv⟩

I hopyd well whan I began
and sens the proue is contrary.
why shold I any longer than.
couet that thing that wyll not be.

But rather to leaue now at the last.
then styll to folowe fanzy.
content with the payn that is past
and not couet that thing that will not be.

Finis.